Elizabeth Baird's Favourites

150 Classic Canadian Recipes

James Lorimer & Company, Publishers
Toronto 1984

ISBN 0-88862-759-9 cloth
0-88862-758-0 paper

Cover design: Don Fernley.
Cover photo: Fred Bird.
Food stylist: Kate Bush.

The dishes shown on the front cover, from left to right, are: Cheddar Cheese Bread, Aromatic Roast Chicken, Red Pepper and Eggplant Caviar, Raspberry Lemon Cream Pie, Fall Greens with Garlic Yogurt Dressing, and Red Pepper and Broccoli Salad.

Canadian Cataloguing in Publication Data

Baird, Elizabeth, 1939-
Elizabeth Baird's favourites: 150 great Canadian recipes

(Great Canadian recipes)
Includes index.

1. Cookery, Canadian. I. Title. II. Series.

TX715.B34 1984 641.5971 C84-099246-7

James Lorimer & Company, Publishers
Egerton Ryerson Memorial Building
35 Britain Street
Toronto, Ontario M5A 1R7

Printed and bound in Canada

6 5 4 3 2 1 84 85 86 87 88 89

For George

CONTENTS

ACKNOWLEDGEMENTS

Writing a book is never a solo job, and this is especially true of cookbooks. My thanks go to all who have shared their wealth of knowledge about, and great love for, food. Many have been generous in providing me with their prized recipes. I am always touched by this trait in good cooks.

For the help of Sandy Hall with testing recipes, of Elizabeth Barry, Sheila Cumberland, Rose Murray, Rhomney Gray, Monda Rosenberg and Arlene Lappin in preparing the manuscript, I am grateful. Rachel van Nostrand kindly lent her wonderful country kitchen for the cover photo. The staff of James Lorimer & Company have always made the creation of my cookbooks as smooth as possible.

I will always appreciate the opportunity Bonnie Cornell and Shelley Robertson of the *Toronto Star* have afforded me with my weekly column, "Canadian Cookbook". Special thanks go to Carol Ferguson and Marg Fraser of *Canadian Living* for the opportunities they too have given me. Many of the dishes I first made for "Canadian Cookbook" and *Canadian Living* have become true favourites, and are included in this volume.

Finally, I gratefully acknowledge the assistance of the Ontario Arts Council.

INTRODUCTION

Cooking is not simply a matter of fixing food for nourishment. It's a creative act, imbued with love. For me, there's no way to separate food from the people who create it—or the people we enjoy it with.

So it was no surprise that memories crowded my mind as I chose my favourite recipes for this book.

I remembered how great cooks like Stella Nedovich, Rachel van Nostrand, Katie Williams and Anita Goldberg welcomed me into their kitchens and shared their special recipes. Their creations come straight from the heart, from years of testing and adding just a dash more of this, a sprinkle of that.

And there were tantalizing memories of tastes created in my own kitchen when Cynthia Coop, Anna Kapelos, Kim Redstone, Tanya Sterioff and Marja Gates came to cook with me. The hours spent chopping, kneading, rolling, sautéing, simmering and folding flashed by, with only the remembrance of a spoonful of minty bean soup or tangy marinated herring fillets lingering on.

Finally, I remembered remarkable meals: the golden glow after a spring dinner at Serge Bruyère's table in Quebec City; the delicious morsels at Barbara Gordon's stylish La Cachette in Vancouver; the explosion of tastes at Winnipeg's Mandarin Restaurant; and casual summer evenings spent savouring barbecued souvlakias, watching the world pass by along the Danforth in Toronto.

If food reveals something about the people who make it, it also reflects the produce available in a country and the cooking traditions that have flourished there. In all my cooking, collecting, writing and teaching, my goal has been to keep alive the best of our pioneer cooking traditions and to make the most of Canada's own produce.

But keeping the traditions alive is not enough. It is now time to expand on them, exploring new ways of cooking Canada's berries, peppers, whitefish, beef and Cheddar. Canadian cooking can't be an archival approach to food; to be a true cuisine, Canadian cooking has to draw its inspiration from all the possibilities of the foods we produce and from all the people who make Canada their home. This is why I've included recipes such as squash and leek soup with ginger, curried beef balls, Ellis Galea's aromatic roast chicken, Bungees' wild rice and blueberry pudding and pane dulce di Pasqua. They're all part of Canadian cooking.

Since I love to cook, some of my favourite dishes are the kind I prepare when a full glorious day in the kitchen stretches before me. Many of the relishes, chutneys and marmalades fit into this category. But, like everyone else, I need dishes that are quick and easy, and many of the recipes in this book are just that. But I don't rely on mixes to save time: my favourites come to the table tasting terrific because of their natural fresh ingredients, whether the preparation time is 30 minutes or 3 hours.

It's my pleasure to share some of my favourite recipes with you. I hope they'll become your favourites too.

Elizabeth Baird

APPETIZERS

In the last two decades the humble appetizer has been elevated to a position of culinary importance. World travel and the food writing explosion have opened our eyes to the delights of dividing our meals, especially when entertaining, into several small courses. The one big plateful is definitely passé. Then too, inviting friends over for drinks and hors d'oeuvre is a relaxing way to entertain.

For the big party in any season, make savoury appetizers such as the taramasalata, smoked whitefish pâté, marinated herring or golden caviar hors d'oeuvre in advance and keep them in the refrigerator until your first guests arrive. These finger foods are easy to eat on crisp crackers, thinly sliced black bread or crunchy romaine lettuce hearts. For pleasant summer barbecues, you might like the spicy beef kebabs dipped into a cucumber and yogurt dressing or popped into pita rounds. Deep-fried appetizers, such as the eggplant and zucchini fritters and the deep-fried Camembert, are irresistible, but are best reserved for those get-togethers where the cook can easily slip into the kitchen to do some last-minute frying.

I like to serve the asparagus tartlets and the smothered scallops with cucumbers at plate-and-fork occasions. That usually means a sit-down dinner, though most of the preparation for these two can be done ahead.

Of course the simplest appetizer at any meal is a serving of fresh or crunchy cooked vegetables with herbs, lemon and butter. Green vegetables are the best; asparagus, beans, sugar snap or snow peas, Brussels sprouts, zucchini and broccoli are among my favourites for simple family dinners or easy entertaining.

Asparagus Tartlets

12 tart shells, pricked and baked until lightly browned	12
1 lb asparagus (1 bunch)	500 g
3 tbsp unsalted butter	50 mL
1 tbsp flour	15 mL
1 cup whipping cream	250 mL
½ tsp salt	2 mL
Pinch each freshly ground pepper and nutmeg	Pinch
1 cup grated Gruyère cheese (3 oz/100 g)	250 mL

Serge Bruyère, chef-owner of "à la table de Serge Bruyère", in Quebec City, is the source of this recipe. Bruyère arranges the asparagus pieces in a large pie shell, drenches them in a rich cream sauce and finally sprinkles Gruyère cheese on top. For a more attractive serving at home, bake the filling in individual quiche or tart shells.

Trim asparagus. Wash and place upright in a tall saucepan. Pour in about 1 inch (2.5 cm) of boiling water; cover and cook until tender, about 6 minutes. Drain and cut asparagus into 1-inch (2.5 cm) lengths and set aside.

Meanwhile, in a heavy saucepan, melt butter over low heat. Add flour and cook, stirring, for 2 minutes without browning. Pour in cream and season with salt, pepper and nutmeg. Whisking constantly, bring to a gentle boil. Cook for 2 minutes, stirring to make a smooth sauce. Remove from heat.

(If preparing ahead, bake shells, cook and refrigerate asparagus and make sauce. Float a thin layer of cream on the surface of the sauce to prevent a skin from forming.)

When it is time to serve the tartlets, fill the shells with asparagus. Stir sauce and spoon over asparagus; sprinkle with cheese.

Bake at 375°F (190°C) until sauce is bubbly and cheese is melted, about 10 minutes. Serve immediately on warmed plates. Guests will need forks.

Makes 12 appetizer-sized tartlets.

Note: When the asparagus season is over, you can substitute broccoli cooked just until tender. An old white Cheddar cheese can be used in place of Gruyère.

Sesame Cheddar Rounds

1 cup all-purpose flour	250 mL
1/4 tsp salt	1 mL
Pinch each cayenne and paprika	Pinch
1/3 cup cold butter	75 mL
1/2 cup grated old white Cheddar cheese	125 mL
1 egg, separated	1
2 tbsp (approx) cold water	25 mL
2 tbsp sesame seeds	25 mL

Old Cheddar cheese gives this long-time favourite party snack real zip. These crispy cheesy rounds go especially well with a glass of dry sherry.

In a bowl, combine flour, salt, cayenne and paprika. With a pastry blender or 2 knives, cut in butter until the mixture has the consistency of rolled oats. Stir in cheese.

Whisk together egg yolk and water and sprinkle over dry ingredients. With a fork, stir and press together, adding a bit more water if necessary to form dough. Shape into a ball with your fingers.

(Alternatively, combine flour, salt, cayenne and paprika in a food processor; cut in the butter. Add cheese, then egg yolk and water and process until combined.)

Roll out dough on a lightly floured counter to 1/8-inch (3 mm) thickness. Use a 1 3/4-inch (4 cm) cutter to cut dough into rounds. If you're in a hurry, simply cut pastry into diamonds.

Using a fork, beat egg white until foamy and brush over pastry. Sprinkle evenly with sesame seeds and transfer to a lightly greased baking sheet.

Bake at 400°F (200°C) for 8 to 10 minutes or until golden brown. Let cool on a rack and store in airtight container or freeze for longer storage. Reheat briefly before serving in a napkin-lined basket.

Makes about 36 rounds.

Red Pepper and Eggplant Caviar with Chèvre Cream Spread

2 sweet red bell peppers (each 6 oz/150 g)	2
2 sweet yellow bell peppers (each 6 oz/150 g)	2
1 eggplant (about ¾ lb/375 g)	1
1 tomato	1
2 large cloves garlic, minced	2
2 tbsp chopped Italian parsley	25 mL
¼ cup olive oil	50 mL
1 tbsp lemon juice	15 mL
1 tbsp red wine vinegar	15 mL
½ tsp salt	2 mL
Pinch freshly ground pepper	Pinch

CHÈVRE CREME SPREAD:

½ cup cream cheese	125 mL
½ cup chèvre (goats) cream cheese	125 mL

Spread this creamy cheese mixture over Melba toast (homemade if possible) and top with red pepper and eggplant relish. Use a soft European-style cream cheese, the kind you can buy in bulk in delicatessens and some grocery stores.

Wash peppers and eggplant; dry. Broil 4 inches from heat for 5 to 8 minutes per side or until blistered. Don't worry if skins char somewhat but avoid excessive burning. Pop into a plastic bag and let steam for 10 minutes to loosen skins. Peel, removing all seeds. If eggplant appears watery, drain in a sieve for a few minutes. Peel and seed tomato.

Chop all vegetables into ¼-inch (5 mm) cubes and transfer to a bowl. Stir in remaining ingredients. Taste and adjust seasoning if necessary. If possible, let stand for 1 to 2 hours to mellow flavours. Taste again before serving.

SPREAD: Blend together both cheeses and serve in a pretty bowl with Melba toast and caviar.

Makes 8 appetizing servings.

Beef Kebabs

¼ cup butter	50 mL
⅔ cup finely chopped onion (1 medium)	150 mL
2 cloves garlic, minced	2
1 tsp cumin	5 mL
1 lb finely ground lean beef or lamb	500 g
⅓ cup finely chopped pecans	75 mL

Tiny spicy kebabs make great appetizers cooked outdoors over the coals or indoors under the grill. Serve as is with cucumber sauce or form them into mini-patties and stuff into tiny pita rounds, split and warmed along side the meat.

In a small saucepan, melt butter and sauté onion, garlic and cumin over low heat for 4 to 5 minutes to develop flavours. In a large bowl, combine onion mixture with all the remain-

2 tbsp finely chopped fresh mint	25 mL
1 tsp salt	5 mL
½ tsp curry powder	2 mL
Pinch cayenne	Pinch
1 egg	1

YOGURT CUCUMBER SAUCE:

1 cup natural yogurt	250 mL
1 tsp lemon juice	5 mL
¼ cup grated, peeled seeded cucumber	50 mL

ing ingredients for the kebabs and mix until ingredients are well blended.

For kebabs, wet hands and form meat mixture into rounds or ovals, using a rounded tablespoon (15 mL) of meat at a time. (It helps to dip your hands in cold water to keep them from sticking to the meat.) Thread kebabs onto skewers. If forming into patties, flatten. Refrigerate if preparing ahead.

Grill meat about 3 inches (8 cm) from the heat for 3 to 4 minutes on each side. Serve with Yogurt Cucumber Sauce or in pita rounds with chutney.

SAUCE: Combine all ingredients and keep chilled until serving. Spoon sauce over patties.

Makes about 30 mini-kebabs or patties.

Mussel Salad Appetizer

24 large mussels, about 2½ lb (1.25 kg)	24
4 tsp liquid from steaming the mussels	20 mL
⅔ cup mayonnaise, preferably homemade	150 mL
2 tsp finely chopped fresh parsley	10 mL
1 tsp lemon juice	5 mL
¼ tsp curry powder	1 mL
Pinch cayenne	Pinch
1 head Boston lettuce, washed and dried	1
4 to 6 sprigs fresh coriander or parsley	4 to 6
1 cantaloupe	1

Dress steamed Maritime cultured mussels with a mild curry mayonnaise. Serve as an appetizer or light lunch in a cup of Boston lettuce garnished with a wedge of cantaloupe.

In a large saucepan, place mussels in about 1 inch (2.5 cm) of water. Bring to a boil, cover and steam until mussels open, about 6 minutes. Discard any that don't open. Drain, reserving 4 tsp (20 mL) of liquid, and let cool.

Shell mussels, open the meats slightly and remove any remnants of the beard (byssus). Place in a large bowl with remaining ingredients except lettuce, coriander and melon. Mix gently but thoroughly. Taste and add salt if necessary (usually the mussels and mayonnaise are salty enough). Cover and chill until serving time.

Carefully separate lettuce into individual leaves. Scoop mussels into lettuce cups. Garnish with coriander. Peel and seed melon; cut into 12 wedges to garnish plates.

Makes 4 servings as a light lunch, 6 as an appetizer.

Three-Day Three-Onion Marinated Herring

3 whole salt herring	3
$1\frac{1}{4}$ cups water	300 mL
$\frac{2}{3}$ cup white vinegar	150 mL
$\frac{2}{3}$ cup granulated sugar	150 mL
1 medium white cooking onion	1
1 medium red onion	1
1 medium leek, green part only	1
1 medium carrot	1
6 bay leaves	6
$\frac{1}{2}$ tsp mustard seed	2 mL
10 whole allspice	10
10 whole cloves	10
10 whole white peppercorns	10

From the Finnish Christmas Eve buffet of Torontonian Marja Gates comes this wonderfully piquant herring. You'll have to plan ahead: it takes one day to soak the herring, and at least two more to marinate it with red onions, carrots and leeks. It's as handsome in the jar as it is good in the mouth.

Look for salt herring at fishmongers or delicatessens that specialize in European foods.

Soak herring for 12 to 24 hours in cold water to cover, changing water 2 or 3 times. With a very sharp knife, fillet herring, always keeping knife pointed towards the interior and making short cutting strokes. Clean stomach; leave skin attached. Cut into 1-inch (2.5 cm) pieces.

Combine water, vinegar and sugar in a small saucepan. Bring to a boil, stirring constantly until sugar is dissolved. Let cool to room temperature.

Meanwhile, thinly slice onions and leek. Cut carrot thinly on the diagonal.

In a glass bowl or wide-mouthed jar with approximately 8-cup (2 L) capacity, layer herring with vegetables and spices. Pour cooled pickling liquid over, cover and marinate for at least 2 days in the refrigerator.

To serve, arrange drained herring and vegetables in a glass bowl or, if the marinating jar is attractive, serve herring chunks straight from the jar. Serve some of the onion rings, leek slices and carrots with each bit of herring, but leave liquid in receptacle.

Serves 12 herring aficianados generously. Non-aficianados don't know what they're missing.

Smothered Scallops and Cucumbers

1 tbsp butter	15 mL
2 tbsp finely chopped shallots or onion	25 mL
2 cups peeled, seeded, chopped tomatoes (3 medium)	500 mL
$\frac{1}{4}$ tsp salt	1 mL
Pinch each freshly ground pepper and nutmeg	Pinch
$\frac{1}{2}$ large field cucumber	$\frac{1}{2}$
1 lb scallops, preferably fresh	500 g
$\frac{1}{3}$ cup whipping cream	75 mL
1 tsp finely chopped fresh tarragon or $\frac{1}{2}$ tsp (2 mL) crumbled dried	5 mL
Pinch salt	Pinch
6 sprigs fresh coriander	6

This is an impressive appetizer that Barbara Gordon serves at La Cachette in Vancouver. Most of the dish can be prepared well in advance and needs only a last-minute flash in the pan. Follow Gordon's dictum: use only fully ripe, red tomatoes.

In a medium skillet, melt butter; add the shallots and sauté gently for 3 to 4 minutes or until translucent. Add tomatoes, $\frac{1}{4}$ tsp (1 mL) salt, pepper and nutmeg. Cook, uncovered, over moderate heat, stirring frequently, for 12 minutes or until vegetables are tender and almost all the liquid has evaporated. Remove from heat and set aside.

Peel cucumber; cut in half lengthwise and scoop out the seeds with a spoon. Cut cucumber into medium julienne strips $1\frac{1}{2}$ x $\frac{1}{4}$ inches (4 cm x 5 mm). Place in a medium saucepan of boiling salted water and as soon as the water returns to a boil, drain and rinse thoroughly in cold water. Drain again and keep chilled until needed. Recipe can be prepared to this point up to 8 hours in advance.

Slice the scallops into $\frac{1}{4}$-inch (5 mm) medallions. If using frozen scallops, save 2 tbsp (25 mL) of the juice that forms as they melt. This can be done up to 8 hours in advance, covered and chilled.

Just before serving, pour the cream and scallop liquid, if available, into a large skillet with a tightly fitting lid. Add tarragon, pinch of salt, tomato sauce and cucumber and bring to a simmer over medium heat, stirring to blend the flavours. Increase the heat almost to high and add the scallops. Cover and cook for $1\frac{1}{2}$ minutes, shaking the pan and stirring scallops 2 or 3 times as they cook. Replace lid quickly each time.

Serve scallops and a portion of the sauce immediately in heated dishes and garnish with a sprig of fresh coriander.

Makes 6 appetizer-sized portions.

Smoked Whitefish Pâté

1 smoked whitefish (10 inches/25 cm)	1
⅔ cup mayonnaise, homemade if possible	150 mL
1 tbsp finely chopped onion	15 mL
1 tbsp finely chopped celery	15 mL
½ tsp lemon juice	2 mL
Salt (optional)	
Parsley sprigs	

At the Bay Fish Company in Port Dover, Ontario, the refrigerated cases are stocked with a variety of smoked fish — lake trout, salmon, chub, whitefish and rainbow trout. Jack Powell uses corn cobs to hot-smoke the fish, some of which is caught locally. His main problem is keeping up with the demand. Serve a pot of pâté with crackers or buttered whole wheat toast fingers.

Skin and bone fish. Break into coarse chunks; there should be about 2 cups (500 mL). By hand or with a food processor or blender, mash fish and blend in mayonnaise, onion, celery and lemon juice. Taste and add salt if necessary (smoked fish is usually brined first and is often salty enough).

Transfer pâté to a serving bowl and garnish with parsley.

Makes enough pâté for 8.

Taramasalata

6 slices Mediterranean-style bread (½ inch/1 cm thick)	6
1 cup cold water	250 mL
½ cup tarama	125 mL
¼ cup fresh lemon juice	50 mL
¼ cup finely chopped onion	50 mL
1 clove garlic, minced	1
¾ cup (approx) olive oil	175 mL

Carp roe, the inexpensive ingredient that gives this dip its lusty flavour, is available in jars from specialty shops and Greek grocers. A bowl of taramasalata surrounded by black olives, hearts of romaine and celery sticks is a handsome and welcome appetizer when entertaining a crowd.

Trim crusts from bread. In a medium bowl, soak bread in water for 5 minutes. Transfer to a colander and firmly press out all water.

Place bread, tarama, lemon juice, onion, garlic and ½ cup (125 mL) of the oil in a food processor or blender and process until smooth. With machine running, add more oil until taramasalata holds its shape solidly on a spoon. Taste and add more lemon juice if desired. Pack into a serving bowl.

Makes about 2½ cups (625 mL), enough for starters for 8 friends. Count on about 32 pieces of romaine heart leaves and/or celery sticks for dipping up a whole batch.

Victoria Myers' Caviar Hors d'Oeuvre

12 eggs, at room temperature	12	
1/4 cup finely chopped green onion	50 mL	
3/4 cup (approx) mayonnaise	175 mL	
1/2 tsp salt	2 mL	
1/4 tsp freshly ground pepper	1 mL	
1/4 tsp dry mustard	1 mL	
7 oz caviar, golden whitefish recommended	200 g	
1 cup sour cream	250 mL	
1/3 cup finely chopped fresh parsley	75 mL	

A big glass bowl of caviar and chopped egg with a sour cream topping is a popular hors d'oeuvre when Victoria Myers gives a party in her Yorkville townhouse. Serve with Melba toast, thin slices of dark rye or pumpernickel spread with unsalted butter. It's a terrific make-ahead party dish; in fact, it's better after mellowing for a day in the refrigerator.

To hard-cook the eggs, place them in a single layer in a saucepan. Cover with enough water to come 1 inch (2.5 cm) above the eggs. Bring to a boil, then immediately cover and remove from heat. Let stand for 20 minutes, then drain and cover with 3 generous changes of cold water to cool completely. Crack and peel, using cold water to help ease off the shells.

Chop eggs coarsely and combine with onion, mayonnaise, salt, pepper and mustard. Add more mayonnaise and salt if desired. Spoon into a glass bowl and smooth the surface.

Spread caviar over the egg salad, then layer sour cream evenly over the caviar. Cover and refrigerate for up to 1 day.

To serve, sprinkle parsley in a ring around the edge of the bowl. Let guests spoon the caviar and eggs onto Melba toast, making sure they get all three layers for a complete range of taste and texture.

Enough for 10 very generous servings.

Eggplant Fritters

1½ lb eggplant, finger-sized if possible, or zucchini	750 g
1 tbsp salt	15 mL
⅓ cup all-purpose flour	75 mL
Oil for deep-frying	

BATTER:

1 cup all-purpose flour	250 mL
¼ tsp salt	1 mL
1 cup (approx) soda water	250 mL
2 tbsp oil	25 mL
2 egg whites	2

Farmers' markets have mushroomed across the country and one of the new ones can be found every summer Friday in the parking lot at Square One in Mississauga, Ontario. The flat black pavement fills up with orderly rows of trucks soon surrounded by seemingly endless quantities of apples, peaches, plums and pears, bushels of beans and tomatoes, and baskets of corn cobs. One visit in late August turned up superb eggplant — bulbous, dark purple ones from Punjab Farms; round, pale green ones; slim, thin-skinned purple ones with mauve and white streaks from Naka Greenhouses; purple specimens the size of a baby's fist; and finger-sized Italian eggplant. Inspired by them all, I went home to prepare them in a way suggested by one of the shoppers — fritters that capture the delicate, nutty, sweet taste of eggplant in a light crisp batter. Zucchini also makes superb fritters.

Cut small eggplant (or zucchini) lengthwise into ⅓-inch (1 cm) thick slices. If using large eggplant, slice it crosswise, then cut each slice in half to form half moons. Layer with salt in a large colander. Let drain for 1 to 2 hours.

BATTER: Combine all ingredients for the batter except the egg whites. Cover and let stand for 1 to 2 hours at room temperature.

Pat eggplant slices dry with paper towels. Spread ⅓ cup (75 mL) flour in a shallow pan and coat the slices on both sides with flour. Shake off excess.

Beat egg whites to soft peaks and fold into batter. The batter should have the consistency of natural yogurt; add a little more soda water if necessary.

Dip eggplant slices, one at a time, in the batter, letting excess batter drip back into the bowl. In a deep fryer or heavy saucepan, heat 3 inches (8 cm) oil to 360°F (185°C) and deep-fry fritters, without crowding, until puffed and golden. Drain on crumpled paper towels and serve immediately.

Makes 6 servings as a side dish, more if served as an appetizer.

Deep-fried Camembert or Brie

8 oz chilled Camembert or Brie cheese	250 g
2 tbsp flour	25 mL
1 egg	1
1 cup dry, fine (but not powdery) bread crumbs from Mediterranean-style bread	250 mL
Oil for deep-frying	

Leona Chase made her name with cheese at the Cheese Wheel in Toronto. So what could be more natural than for her to feature cheese when she caters to receptions and parties? From Leona Chase's repertoire of cheese hors d'oeuvre, here are Camembert or Brie wedges, deep-fried in a crisp crumb crust and served while the centre is still oozing. Complement with deep-fried parsley or curly endive.

Cut cheese into wedges about 2½ inches (6 cm) long and 1½ inches (4 cm) across. Roll in flour, shaking off excess. Beat egg in a shallow bowl. Using tongs, dip cheese into the egg, then roll in the crumbs to coat wedges completely. Sprinkle remaining crumbs onto a small tray and set the wedges on the crumbs. Chill for 1 to 3 hours.

Deep-fry cheese in 2 inches (5 cm) of oil heated to 350°F (180°C) for about 1½ minutes on each side. Drain on paper towels.

Makes about 8 wedges.

SOUPS

The word "soup" brings to mind ease, economy — and even elegance. In the summer, take the simple but stylish route with the make-ahead black cherry and wine soup, the easy carrot soup or the summer garden soup with almonds. They are great starters at any smart Sunday supper, and all are naturally colourful: think pink for the cherry, delicate orange for the carrot and a medley of reds and greens garnishing the creamy white cucumber of the summer soup.

Generations of Canadians have appreciated the restorative quality of hearty soups that warm and comfort. In this category there's Cynthia Coop's bean and barley soup with wild mushrooms, the cod and shrimp chowder, the tomato mushroom soup with croutons and "bop" (white bean and pepper soup). For one-dish suppers, serve with a tossed garden salad and a crusty loaf — Mediterranean-style, dark rye or whole wheat. Soups like these suit a busy family; they are perfect for when the gang drops in and easy to reheat in individual portions.

For ease and economy, look to vegetable potages: the speedy Kingsway broccoli or the squash and leek soup with ginger are inexpensive soups that can be made in minutes without sacrificing taste.

Black Cherry and Wine Soup

⅓ cup granulated sugar	75 mL
1 cinnamon stick	1
4 whole cloves	4
6 strips lemon peel, the length of a large lemon and ½ inch (1 cm) wide	6
½ cup strained lemon juice	125 mL
1 bottle (750 mL) fruity dry white wine, Riesling suggested	1

A cold fruit soup — cherry is one of the best — is a first rate way to begin a summer picnic or patio supper. For a tarter version, use sour red cherries instead of sweet black ones.

In a medium saucepan, combine sugar, cinnamon stick, cloves, lemon peel, juice and wine. Bring to a boil; add cherries and bring back to a boil. Reduce heat and simmer, uncovered, for about 5 minutes or until cherries are barely tender.

Let cool, then remove and discard cinnamon stick, cloves

4 cups pitted black cherries (1½ lb/750 g)	1 L
2 cups sour cream	500 mL
½ cup whipping cream	125 mL

and lemon peel. Set aside 16 of the finest cherries. Purée remaining cherries and liquid until smooth. Add sour cream and whipping cream.

Chill, taste and adjust sugar or lemon juice. Serve in chilled goblets with 2 whole cherries floating on top of each serving.

Makes 8 rich servings.

Summer Garden Soup with Almonds

Susan Thompson of Toronto introduced me to this creamy cucumber soup with garden garnishes, and it has rapidly become an entertaining favourite. Every guest has a bowl of the basic chilled soup and adds chopped tomatoes, red or green peppers, green onions, parsley and toasted almonds to please themselves. This is a soup to keep in mind when you want to entertain without last-minute fussing.

1½ long slim greenhouse cucumbers or 3 medium field cucumbers	1½
3 cups cold chicken stock (see page 60)	750 mL
3 cups sour cream	750 mL
1 clove garlic, minced	1
3 tbsp white wine vinegar	50 mL
1 tsp salt	5 mL

GARNISH:

¾ cup sliced almonds	175 mL
1½ cups chopped, peeled, seeded tomatoes (3 medium)	375 mL
½ cup sliced green onions	125 mL
½ cup finely chopped fresh parsley, preferably Italian	125 mL
½ cup finely chopped red or green bell pepper	125 mL

Peel greenhouse cucumbers; peel and seed field variety. Either grate coarsely and blend with the stock, or cube coarsely and chop in a food processor or blender with 1 cup (250 mL) of the stock, then transfer to a large bowl and add remaining stock.

Stir in sour cream, garlic, vinegar and salt and chill. Taste and adjust seasoning when soup is cold.

GARNISH: Toast almonds at 350°F (180°C) for 10 minutes, stirring periodically to brown slices evenly; let cool. Place garnishes in separate bowls. Cover vegetables and keep cool until serving time.

Pour soup into a large chilled tureen and arrange garnishes nearby. Ladle soup into bowls and serve (glass bowls make pretty receptacles for this soup). Let guests choose their own garnishes.

Makes 8 generous servings.

Speedy Kingsway Broccoli Soup

3 tbsp butter	50 mL
¼ cup chopped onion or shallots	50 mL
¼ cup chopped celery	50 mL
1 lb broccoli (1 bunch)	500 g
½ cup chicken stock	125 mL
1 cup cream, light or whipping	250 mL
½ tsp salt	2 mL
¼ tsp curry powder	1 mL
Pinch freshly ground pepper	Pinch

A recipe from the kitchen of Mary Patterson, super mother, teacher and cook in Toronto's elegant west end. Patterson serves this soup hot or cold with a dollop of sour cream. She finds it's special enough for buffets or sit-down dinner parties, yet quick enough for a last-minute lunch.

In a heavy medium saucepan, melt butter; add onion and celery and fry gently for 5 minutes.

Trim ends from broccoli stalks and peel coarse outer skin. Chop into 1-inch (2.5 cm) lengths and break florets into 2-inch (5 cm) clumps. Add broccoli and stock to pan and stir. Cover and simmer for 10 to 15 minutes or just until broccoli is tender. Beware of overcooking broccoli; it loses its fresh taste.

Purée soup in a food mill, processor or blender and return it to the saucepan. Add remaining ingredients and heat through. Taste, adjust seasoning if desired and add more cream or even milk if a thinner soup suits your preferences.

To serve cold, chill and adjust seasoning.

Makes 4 generous lunch-sized servings, 6 more modest dinner-party portions. Recipe can be doubled.

Easy Parsnip Soup (Easy Carrot Soup Too)

6 cups chicken stock (see page 60)	1.5 L
1 stalk celery	1
1½ cups coarsely chopped onions (2 medium)	375 mL
1 lb parsnips (8 medium) or carrots	500 g
½ tsp coarsely grated orange peel	2 mL

Parsnips have, of recent years, been underappreciated. Too many soggy servings have hidden the wonderful possibilities of this root. Take advantage of winter and spring parsnips to make this pale but full-flavoured soup, flecked with parsley and a hint of orange. For carrot soup, simply substitute carrots for the parsnips.

Pour stock into a large saucepan. Pull strings from celery; slice celery coarsely and add to stock along with onions.

¼ tsp freshly grated nutmeg	1 mL
Salt and freshly ground pepper	

GARNISH:

⅓ cup chopped fresh parsley or chervil	75 mL
¼ cup sour cream or natural yogurt	50 mL

Peel parsnips; chop and add to stock. Cover and bring to a boil; reduce heat and simmer until vegetables are tender, about 30 minutes.

Purée soup in a food processor and return to a clean saucepan. (If you use a food mill to purée the vegetables, it is not necessary to remove strings from the celery.) Add orange peel and nutmeg and season with salt and pepper. Bring to a simmer.

Serve soup in warmed soup bowls. Scatter about 1 tbsp (15 mL) parsley over each bowl and add about 2 tsp (10 mL) sour cream in one dollop.

Diners can swirl the parsley and cream into their soup.

Makes 6 servings.

Sorrel and Spinach Soup

2 tbsp butter	25 mL
1½ cups chopped spinach, stems removed	375 mL
½ cup chopped fresh sorrel, stems removed	125 mL
4 cups chicken stock (see page 60)	1 L
3 egg yolks	3
½ cup whipping cream	125 mL
Salt and freshly ground pepper	
2 tbsp chopped fresh chervil or parsley	25 mL

This spring soup was inspired by a visit to the Richter greenhouses near Goodwood, Ontario. Amidst the Richters' cornucopia of herbs, you'll find sorrel, with its spade-shaped, bright green leaves. It adds a special tang to any soup or salad. If sorrel isn't available, substitute two tablespoons (25 mL) of fresh dill.

In a medium saucepan, melt butter over medium heat. Add spinach and sorrel and cook, stirring, until leaves wilt, about 1 minute.

Pour in stock and bring to a boil. Reduce heat and simmer, uncovered, for 3 to 4 minutes. Whisk together the egg yolks and cream. Blend about ½ cup (125 mL) of the hot soup into the yolk mixture. Gradually stir the mixture into the soup.

Cook, stirring constantly, over medium heat for 3 to 5 minutes or until slightly thickened. Taste and add salt and pepper.

Pour into warmed soup bowls, garnish with a touch of chervil and serve immediately. Or chill and serve in stemmed glasses.

Makes 4 or 5 servings.

Tomato Mushroom Soup with Croutons

$\frac{1}{4}$ cup butter	50 mL
1 large clove garlic, minced	1
1 cup finely chopped onion (1 large)	250 mL
$1\frac{1}{2}$ cups sliced mushrooms (4 oz/125 g)	375 mL
4 tsp flour	20 mL
4 cups chopped, peeled fresh tomatoes or canned, undrained	1 L
4 cups chicken stock (see page 60)	1 L
2 tsp granulated sugar	10 mL
$\frac{1}{2}$ tsp finely chopped fresh basil or $\frac{1}{4}$ tsp (1 mL) crumbled dried	2 mL
$\frac{1}{2}$ tsp finely chopped fresh rosemary or $\frac{1}{4}$ tsp (1 mL) crumbled dried	2 mL
Pinch chopped fresh or crumbled dried thyme	Pinch
Freshly ground pepper	
Salt	

CROUTONS:

$\frac{1}{4}$ cup butter	50 mL
1 clove garlic, slivered	1
2 slices homemade whole wheat or white bread, cut in $\frac{1}{2}$-inch (1 cm) cubes	2

Good the day it's made, even better reheated the next day and garnished with buttery crisp croutons. In the summer use fresh tomatoes; in the winter, canned.

In a large saucepan, melt butter over medium heat; add garlic and onion and sauté for 3 to 4 minutes. Add mushrooms and sauté for 4 minutes longer or until vegetables are tender. Stir in flour; cook for 2 minutes without browning.

Stir in tomatoes, stock, sugar, basil, rosemary, thyme and pepper. Bring to a boil; reduce heat and simmer, partially covered, for 45 minutes. Taste and add salt, more herbs and a touch of sugar if needed.

CROUTONS: In a medium skillet, melt butter over medium heat. Add garlic and sauté for 3 to 4 minutes. Add bread cubes, stirring to let them soak up the butter, and sauté until golden and crisp, about 5 minutes. Watch carefully that garlic doesn't burn or croutons brown too deeply. Remove and discard garlic.

To serve, pour soup into warmed soup bowls and top with croutons.

Makes 6 hearty servings.

Cynthia Coop's Bean and Barley Soup with Wild Mushrooms

$1\frac{1}{4}$ lb	chuck steak	625 g
$1\frac{3}{4}$ lb	beef shank slices	875 g
$1\frac{3}{4}$ lb	beef marrow bones	875 g
20 cups	cold water	5 L
3 cups	chopped celery, stalks and leaves (4 stalks)	750 mL
2 cups	coarsely chopped onions (4 medium)	500 mL
$1\frac{1}{2}$ cups	coarsely chopped carrots (3 medium)	375 mL
15 stalks	fresh parsley	15
5 sprigs	fresh dill, stalks and leaves (not seed heads)	5
1 clove	garlic, quartered	1
2 tsp	salt	10 mL
1 tsp	cracked peppercorns	5 mL
1 cup	navy beans	250 mL
$\frac{1}{2}$ cup	pearl or pot barley	125 mL
5 to 10	dried porcini mushrooms	5 to 10

Winnipeg interior designer Cynthia Coop is a fine cook. This soup, a recipe she learned as a bride from her mother-in-law, is one you can build a reputation on. When the tiny North End Market in Winnipeg has them, Cynthia uses wild mushrooms; otherwise she makes do with imported porcini (cèpe). The strings of dried mushrooms sold in Polish and Ukrainian butcher stores and delicatessens are also excellent for this soup. Dried mushrooms add an indescribable rich, almost musty, flavour to any dish. Once you've tasted them, you'll find cultivated mushrooms insipid.

Rinse meat and bones briefly in cold water. Place in a large stock pot. Pour in cold water and bring to a boil, skimming off all foam.

Add celery, onions and carrots. Tie parsley and dill together and add to the pot with garlic, salt, peppercorns, beans, barley and mushrooms. Bring back to a boil. Reduce heat and simmer, covered, for 3 to 4 hours or until the meat and beans are tender. If time allows, let cool, then chill overnight.

Remove fat, parsley and dill. Scoop out meat and bones. Remove marrow from bones; trim fat from meat. Chop meat and marrow neatly and return to soup.

Heat through. Like all "mother-earth" soups, this is best made a day ahead and reheated. It also freezes well.

Makes 12 to 14 meal-in-one servings.

White Bean and Pepper Soup

1 lb dried white kidney beans	500 g
10 cups cold water	2.5 L
½ cup oil	125 mL
2 cups chopped onions (3 medium-large)	500 mL
2 large sweet banana peppers, seeded and chopped	2
1 large hot banana pepper, seeded and chopped	1
1 large clove garlic, minced	1
4 cups chopped, peeled tomatoes or canned, undrained	1 L
2 tsp salt	10 mL
¼ tsp each freshly ground pepper and paprika	1 mL
¼ cup chopped fresh mint plus extra for garnish	50 mL

Known in Macedonian as *bop*, this thick bean, tomato, onion and pepper soup has an unexpected touch: fresh mint.

Rinse beans; transfer to a large stock pot and soak overnight in three times their depth of water. (Alternatively, quick-soak beans by bringing them to a boil in the above quantity of water and boil, uncovered, for 2 minutes. Cover, remove from heat and let stand for 1 hour.) Drain and rinse beans whichever method used.

Return beans to stock pot; add the 10 cups (2.5 L) water and bring to a simmer; cook gently, uncovered, for 1 to 2 hours or until tender.

Meanwhile, in a large skillet, heat oil; sauté onions, sweet and hot peppers and garlic over medium heat until softened, about 8 minutes. Add tomatoes, salt, pepper and paprika and cook, stirring frequently, for 10 minutes or until mixture is like a sauce. Add to the beans.

Stir in the mint. Bring to a gentle simmer and cook, covered, for about 1 hour longer or until some of the beans have begun to break down to provide a creamy base to the soup.

Taste, adjust seasoning and thin soup if desired with more water.

Ladle into shallow bowls and sprinkle with additional chopped fresh mint.

Makes 8 servings.

Squash and Leek Soup with Ginger

10 cups chicken stock (see page 60)	2.5 L
6 cups chopped butternut or hubbard squash, in ½-inch (1 cm) cubes	1.5 L
1 cup thinly sliced leek (1 medium)	250 mL
1 cup finely chopped onion (1 large)	250 mL
1 tsp ground ginger	5 mL
½ tsp cumin	2 mL
2 tbsp cider vinegar	25 mL
¼ tsp Tabasco sauce	1 mL
⅓ cup finely chopped green onions	75 mL
2 tsp chopped fresh basil or 1 tsp (5 mL) crumbled dried	10 mL

GARNISH:

2 tbsp sesame seeds	25 mL
1 tbsp finely chopped fresh ginger	15 mL

A clear, interestingly spiced soup that's perfect to make in the fall after a visit to a farmers' market.

In a large saucepan or stock pot, combine stock, squash, leek, onion, ginger, cumin, vinegar and Tabasco. Bring to a boil; reduce heat and simmer, partially covered, until squash is tender, about 15 minutes. Skim if necessary. Add green onions and basil and simmer for 5 minutes longer. Taste and adjust seasoning.

Meanwhile, toast sesame seeds until golden in a small skillet over medium heat for 30 to 60 seconds, stirring constantly. Prepare ginger and set aside.

Ladle the soup into shallow, old-fashioned soup bowls. Stir a portion of fresh ginger into each soup bowl and garnish with sesame seeds.

Makes 12 generous servings.

Cod and Shrimp Chowder

When my sister Janey Purvis makes chowder, she uses fresh cod or any firm white ocean fish and adds a few shrimps for colour and flavour. She likes to add a dollop of sour cream at the end, a West Coast variation on an old Canadian soup. To keep the fish from overcooking, Janey Purvis suggests cooking the fish and flavourings in one pot and the potatoes in a second; combine just before serving. It's quicker too.

POT ONE — FISH AND STOCK:

6 cups cold water	1.5 L
1 cup chopped celery, stalks and leaves	250 mL
¾ cup chopped onion (1 medium-large)	175 mL
1½ tsp salt	7 mL
6 peppercorns, crushed	6
1 bay leaf	1
4 parsley stalks	4
1 tsp chopped fresh thyme or ½ tsp (2 mL) crumbled dried	5 mL
4 oz raw shrimps in their shells	125 g
1½ lb fresh cod, halibut or haddock	750 g
2 tbsp butter, softened	25 mL
2 tbsp flour	25 mL

POT TWO — POTATOES AND VEGETABLES:

2 cups chopped potatoes, in ½-inch (1 cm) cubes	500 mL
¾ cup chopped onion (1 large)	175 mL
2 cups boiling water	500 mL
½ tsp salt	2 mL
½ cup chopped celery	125 mL
½ cup freshly shelled or frozen peas	125 mL
1 cup sour cream	250 mL
2 tbsp finely chopped fresh coriander or parsley	25 mL

POT ONE: In a large saucepan, combine cold water, celery, onion, salt, peppercorns, bay leaf, parsley and thyme and bring to a boil. Reduce heat and simmer, uncovered, for 30 minutes. The vegetables and herbs in this water make a tasty poaching stock for the fish. Rinse shrimps; add to the stock and simmer for 3 to 5 minutes or until shrimps are opaque and pink. Remove shrimps; peel and devein. Reserve until just before serving.

Add the fish in one piece to the stock and poach until it flakes, about 5 minutes. Remove fish with a slotted spoon; break into bite-sized chunks and reserve with shrimps.

Strain stock, pressing all liquid from the vegetables, and return stock to saucepan. Blend together butter and flour and whisk into the stock, a large spoonful at a time. Reheat and simmer gently for 5 minutes. Reserve over low heat, whisking periodically.

POT TWO: Meanwhile, in a second saucepan, cook potatoes and onion in the boiling water with salt for 10 to 15 minutes or until potatoes are barely tender. Add celery and peas and cook for 5 minutes. Transfer the contents of this pan to the thickened fish stock. Add the reserved fish and shrimps and heat through. Remove from heat. Stir in sour cream. Taste and adjust seasoning if desired.

Serve immediately in warmed shallow soup bowls, making sure shrimps are equitably shared. Garnish each serving with coriander.

Makes 6 servings.

Chunky Lobster Chowder

1½ cups diced new potatoes (3 medium)	375 mL
¾ cup chopped onion (1 medium-large)	175 mL
1 cup water	250 mL
1 cup chopped cooked lobster meat, in ½-inch (1 cm) chunks	250 mL
½ tsp salt	2 mL
¼ tsp freshly ground pepper	1 mL
2 cups milk	500 mL
½ cup whipping cream	125 mL
¼ cup unsalted butter	50 mL
2 tbsp finely chopped fresh parsley or chervil	25 mL

This country-kitchen chowder is full of chunks of pink lobster, cubed new potatoes and a touch of chervil in a milk broth enriched by butter and cream.

A one pound (500 g) live lobster yields about 1 cup (250 mL) lobster meat, enough for the chowder. Boil the lobster for 20 minutes; remove from the pot and submerge immediately in cold water. This keeps the lobster from over-cooking and drying out in its shell. Refrigerate upside-down until needed. You can substitute freshly cooked lobster bought at a fishmonger's, or cooked shelled frozen lobster available in plastic tubs or cans. One 11.3 oz. (320 g) can yields about 2 cups (500 mL) lobster meat, enough to double the recipe.

In a medium saucepan, combine potatoes, onion and water. Cover and bring to a boil. Reduce heat and simmer for 8 to 10 minutes or until potatoes are softened but not cooked through. Add lobster, salt and pepper and simmer for 5 minutes or until potatoes are tender.

Add milk, cream and butter and heat just to a boil. Ladle into a warm tureen or bowls and sprinkle with parsley. Serve with whole wheat crackers or soda bread.

Makes 4 generous servings. You can substitute chopped shrimps, scallops or salmon for the lobster.

THE MAIN COURSE

The heart of the meal — fish or meat. Once the decision has been made, the accompaniments (appetizers, vegetables and salads) will fall into place. For special occasions, there's Pacific salmon with wild rice and pork loin stuffed with hazelnuts. Equally at home for dinner parties are Savella Stechishin's chicken breasts Kiev style or the poached sole with smoked salmon rolls — wickedly delicious white and pink roll-ups napped in natural juices, cream and wine.

Canadians have embraced the barbecue (figuratively, that is). For those reluctant to turn on the stove from May to November, the choice of what to grill is not limited to steaks or burgers: there are marinated whitefish, butter bread crumbed scallops, salmon steaks, devilishly hot whole chickens and souvlakia in a pita with garlic yogurt sauce. When the snow flies, prepare any of these dishes under the grill in your own kitchen or, if you're a diehard, outside in mittens and parka, with a hood over the coals to keep them lit.

When it comes to full satisfying flavour, I can heartily recommend the ranch steaks; they are well worth the extra preparation. And few meals satisfy cooks and eaters alike more than a stew. The veal with mushrooms and dill is a case in point. On the "sea-side", the mussels and wine duet is an easy-to-make, first-class introduction to our home-grown mussel crop.

Dilled Veal Stew with Mushrooms

The mild flavour of veal is admirably complemented by sautéed mushrooms and fresh dill. Since veal is tender and cooks quickly, you can enjoy this dish in short order.

2 tbsp oil	25 mL
¼ cup butter	50 mL
3 lb lean boneless stewing veal, in 1-inch (2.5 cm) cubes	1.35 kg
1½ cups finely chopped onions (3 medium)	375 mL
1 clove garlic, minced	1

In a large heavy saucepan, heat the oil and half the butter. Add one layer of veal and brown on all sides. Remove and brown remaining veal. Remove veal and melt remaining

1 cup finely chopped carrots (2 medium)	250 mL
3 cups sliced mushrooms (8 oz/250 g)	750 mL
¼ cup each chopped fresh dill and parsley	50 mL
1 bay leaf	1
1 tsp chopped fresh thyme or ½ tsp (2 mL) crumbled dried	5 mL
1 tsp salt	5 mL
¼ tsp freshly ground pepper	1 mL
2 cups chicken stock (see page 60)	500 mL
1½ tbsp each flour and soft butter	20 mL
½ cup whipping cream	125 mL
Dill sprigs	

butter. Cook onions, garlic and carrots over moderate heat for 4 minutes. Add mushrooms and fry for 5 minutes.

Return all the veal to the pan and add chopped dill, parsley, bay leaf, thyme, salt and pepper. Pour in the stock and bring to a boil, stirring up the succulent bits from the bottom of the pan.

Reduce heat and simmer gently, partially covered, until veal is tender, about 1 hour. Blend together flour and soft butter and stir into the stew to thicken juices. (If making ahead, let stew cool at this point and reheat before continuing with recipe.)

Stir in cream, heat through and taste. Add any additional seasoning to suit your palate and garnish with dill sprigs.

Makes 6 generous servings. Noodles or rice make very good companions to veal stew but it is more dramatic to serve it with a giant gougère.

Calves' Liver with Onions

2 tbsp butter	25 mL
1½ cups thinly sliced onions (2 medium)	375 mL
¾ lb calves' liver	375 g
½ tsp salt	2 mL
Freshly ground pepper	
2 tbsp white wine or chicken stock	25 mL
¼ cup finely chopped fresh parsley	50 mL
2 lemon wedges	2

Calves' liver is food for the gods, especially when lightly sautéed with onions in butter, in this updated version of an old classic.

In a large skillet, melt butter over medium-low heat. Add onions and cook gently, stirring frequently, until tender, light golden in colour and mellow-smelling, about 30 minutes. Remove onions from pan and keep warm.

Rinse liver and trim off membranes; pat dry. Increase heat to medium-high and sauté liver for 1 to 2 minutes on each side or until lightly browned on the outside but still pink and juicy inside. Season with salt and pepper and transfer to 2 warmed dinner plates.

Return onions to skillet. Add wine and parsley and heat through, stirring up any succulent brown bits from the bottom of the pan. Spoon sauce over liver and garnish with lemon.

Makes 2 generous and self-indulgent servings.

Curried Beef Balls

I love the idea of turning something quite plain, such as ground beef, into a treat. In a rich brown sauce redolent with ginger and curry spices, beef balls can come to the table for the grandest occasion — or for family dinners. Serve with rice (I recommend basmati for its nutty flavour), a cucumber yogurt salad and a fruit chutney. I can't think of a more delicious introduction to curry than this.

SPICE MIXTURE:

2 tbsp ground coriander	25 mL
1 tbsp crushed poppy seeds	15 mL
1½ tsp salt	7 mL
1 tsp each ground cumin, paprika, turmeric and cayenne	5 mL
½ tsp ground cardamom	2 mL
Pinch each cloves, nutmeg, mace and saffron	Pinch

BEEF BALLS:

2 lb lean ground beef	1 kg
1 egg	1
½ cup very finely chopped onion	125 mL
1 clove garlic, minced	1
½ tsp salt	2 mL
2 tbsp flour	25 mL
2 tbsp (approx) oil	25 mL

SAUCE:

1½ cups finely chopped onions	375 mL
2 cloves garlic, minced	2
2 tbsp grated fresh ginger	25 mL
3¼ cups chopped, peeled fresh tomatoes or one can (28 oz/796 mL), undrained	800 mL
½ cup natural yogurt	125 mL
3 tbsp lemon or lime juice	50 mL
½ cup finely chopped fresh coriander or parsley	125 mL

SPICE MIXTURE: Combine all ingredients and set aside.

BEEF BALLS: Using your hands, mix together beef, egg, onion, garlic, salt and 1 tsp (5 mL) of the spice mixture. Form into 18 balls and roll in the flour.

In a large heavy saucepan, heat oil over medium-high heat and brown balls on all sides. Turn carefully to avoid breaking the balls. Remove balls and set aside. Add more oil to pan if necessary, or drain off all but 2 tbsp (25 mL) fat if beef has been fatty.

SAUCE: To the pan, add onions, garlic, ginger and all the remaining spice mixture. Cook over medium heat, stirring frequently, until onions are translucent and the spice mixture has developed an assertively rich aroma. Return beef balls to pan.

Chop tomatoes if canned and add to the pan with the yogurt and lemon juice. Cover partially, bring to a boil and immediately reduce heat to simmer for 1½ hours, stirring frequently and carefully, until the sauce is a rich brown and the meatballs are tender. Taste and adjust seasoning. Sprinkle with coriander.

Makes 6 generous portions.

Ranch Steaks

2 lb round steak, preferably inside round	1 kg
3 tbsp prepared mustard, preferably Dijon	50 mL
Salt and freshly ground pepper	
2 tbsp flour	25 mL

SAUCE:

1½ cups water or stock	375 mL
2 tsp flour	10 mL

Calgarian Bunny Barss' book *Come'n Get It* is a treasure trove of recipes and stories of the Old West. One of the best dishes is round steak sliced thin and pan-fried.

Trim fat from steaks. Cut fat into cubes and place in a heavy saucepan, skillet or Dutch oven. Fry over medium-high heat until fat is rendered. Discard any unmelted fat and turn off heat while preparing meat.

Slice steak about ⅜-inch (1 cm) thick and into pieces about 5 x 2½ inches (12 x 6 cm). Place steak pieces in one layer on a large cutting board and pound each piece all over on both sides with the edge of a saucer or the flat side of a meat pounder. Hit the steak hard enough to almost break through the meat. Spread mustard on both sides of meat and sprinkle lightly with salt and pepper. Using a sieve, sprinkle half the flour on one side of all the steaks. Pound flour in, this time more gently and turn over. Sprinkle with remaining flour and pound in gently.

Heat fat over medium-high heat and fry steaks one layer at a time until browned, about 2 minutes on each side. Increase heat to high if necessary and do not let them stew. Transfer browned pieces to a heated platter and keep warm in the oven. Drain any excess fat from the pan.

SAUCE: In a jar, shake together water and flour until smooth. Stir into pan, scraping up all the rich brown bits from the bottom. Heat, stirring, until bubbly and thickened. Taste and add seasoning if desired (because mustard is already salty and spiced, additional seasoning may not be necessary). Strain into warm sauce boat and serve with the steaks.

Makes 4 or 5 generous servings.

Sheldrake Boulevard Roast Brisket

1 beef brisket (4 to 5 lb/2 to 2.5 kg)	1
2 tsp paprika	10 mL
1 tsp salt	5 mL
1 tsp freshly ground pepper	5 mL
3 large cloves garlic, minced	3
Boiling water	
10 medium roasting potatoes, peeled	10

All the kids who live on Sheldrake Boulevard in north Toronto know Ellen Blankstein's roast brisket is terrific. In fact it's so popular that other mothers on the street have to make it, and the old-fashioned covered roaster that bakes it best is passed from one family to another. I have modified the recipe slightly to replace a commercial seasoning with garlic.

Set brisket on a rack in a roasting pan. Sprinkle both sides with paprika, salt and pepper. Spread garlic over top. Let stand, uncovered, at room temperature for 2 to 3 hours for flavours to penetrate the meat.

Preheat oven to 475°F (240°C). Roast brisket for 15 to 20 minutes, uncovered, to sear outside. Pour ½ inch (1 cm) boiling water into pan; cover snugly with lid or foil and roast at 350°F (180°C) for 1¼ hours. Uncover and place potatoes around the meat. Re-cover and continue cooking until brisket and potatoes are fork-tender, 1 to 1½ hours longer.

To serve, remove potatoes to a warm serving dish. If a crusty top is your ticket to heaven, turn on the broiler and broil roast just long enough for the top to brown to a crunch. Transfer to a cutting board, cover lightly and let rest for 5 to 10 minutes. Cut very thinly across the grain. Skim any fat from pan juices and serve juices with meat and roasted potatoes. Need I add that horseradish or mustard should be on the table?

Makes 8 generous servings.

Aromatic Roast Chicken

1 capon or roasting chicken, oven-ready at about 6 lb (2.75 g)	1
MARINADE:	
½ cup red wine or sweet red vermouth	125 mL
2 tbsp soy sauce	25 mL
¼ cup water	50 mL
¼ cup very finely chopped onion	50 mL
2 tbsp red wine vinegar	25 mL
2 tbsp brown sugar	25 mL
1 tbsp crushed garlic	15 mL
¾ tsp cinnamon	4 mL
2 tsp coarsely crushed coriander	10 mL
2 tsp chopped fresh thyme or 1 tsp (5 mL) crumbled dried	10 mL
¾ tsp freshly ground black pepper	4 mL
1 tsp whole fennel seed	5 mL
1 tsp drained whole green peppercorns (available in jars or cans)	5 mL
3 bay leaves	3
⅓ cup butter, melted	75 mL
Salt	

One of the intriguing new aspects of Canadian cooking is the increased use of spices. For this roast chicken, Ellis Galea, a Maltese-born Toronto architect, prepares a marinade of fennel, coriander and cinnamon with a hefty dash of garlic and thyme. The chicken is as delicious to eat as the aroma wafting from the oven promises.

Wipe chicken inside and out with a clean damp cloth. Place in a large sturdy plastic bag (a freezer bag is ideal). Combine all ingredients for the marinade except the melted butter and salt and pour into the bag. Close with a twist tie and slosh the marinade all around the chicken. Set bag and chicken in a bowl and refrigerate for 1 day, turning chicken over periodically.

Drain chicken, straining and reserving the marinade. Truss chicken and set on a rack in an open roaster. Wipe off any whole spices. Brush melted butter all over top of chicken.

Roast at 325°F (160°C) for 2½ to 3 hours, basting frequently with the marinade and then the pan juices. The chicken will develop a wonderful brown glaze. Remove from the oven, sprinkle with salt and let rest for about 10 minutes for easy carving.

Makes 6 to 8 generous servings. Very good with rice pilaf and crunchy glazed carrots. Also excellent cold for patio suppers and picnics.

Savella Stechishin's Chicken Breasts Kiev Style

2 large whole chicken breasts	2
¾ cup (approx) butter, preferably unsalted	175 mL
Salt and freshly ground pepper	
2 tbsp flour	25 mL
1 egg	1
2 tbsp water	25 mL
1 cup (approx) fine dry bread crumbs	250 mL

This is my adaptation of one of the standout recipes in Savella Stechishin's *Traditional Ukrainian Cookery*. Mrs. Stechishin's method of pan-frying and baking chicken Kiev eliminates troublesome last-minute deep-frying and the results are superb. Mushrooms with Sour Cream (recipe follows) is a satisfying contrast to the crisp chicken.

Split chicken breasts and debone. Slice each breast horizontally into 2 fillets of equal size. Pound fillets very flat and thin, about 1½ to 2 times larger than they were originally. Cut about ½ cup (125 mL) of the butter into 8 pieces about 2 x ½ x ½ inches (5 x 1 x 1 cm) and freeze until very hard. Sprinkle fillets with salt and pepper and chill while the butter is hardening.

Lay one fillet flat on counter. Place a piece of butter near the widest end of the fillet; fold the end and sides over the butter and roll up neatly, encasing the butter completely. Skewer the opening securely with a toothpick. Roll up remaining 7 breast fillets the same way.

Combine flour with a pinch of salt and pepper. In a shallow bowl, beat together egg and water. Spread bread crumbs in another shallow bowl or pan. Coat rolls with flour mixture, then dip in the egg mixture. Coat with the bread crumbs.

In a large skillet, melt remaining butter. Over medium-high heat, brown the chicken rolls briefly but thoroughly on all sides. Drain and place on a large baking sheet. Bake at 400°F (200°C) for 5 minutes. Remove wooden picks and serve immediately on a hot platter.

Makes 4 rich servings.

Mushrooms with Sour Cream

2 tbsp butter	25 mL
¼ cup finely chopped onion	50 mL
6 cups sliced mushrooms (1 lb/500 g)	1.5 L
2 tbsp flour	25 mL
1 cup sour cream	250 mL
1 small clove garlic, minced	1
Salt and freshly ground pepper	
1 tsp chopped fresh dill	5 mL

This is the best possible sauce for Chicken Breasts Kiev Style.

In a small saucepan, melt butter over medium heat. Add onion and sauté just until wilted, about 2 minutes. Add mushrooms and cook for 5 minutes or until they too are limp.

Blend flour with some of the sour cream to make a smooth paste. Stir in remaining cream and blend into the mushroom mixture. Cook, stirring, until the mixture comes to a simmer. Reduce heat immediately, add garlic and season to taste. Cover and simmer for 5 minutes to blend flavours. Stir in the dill and serve with Savella Stechishin's Chicken Breasts Kiev Style.

Makes 4 servings.

Mandarin Harvest in Snow

HARVEST VEGETABLES:

4 dried Chinese mushrooms		4
¼ cup finely chopped onion		50 mL
¼ cup finely chopped water chestnuts		50 mL
Pinch salt		Pinch
2 tsp light soy sauce		10 mL
1½ tsp rice wine		7 mL
1 tsp Oriental sesame oil		5 mL
1 green onion, finely chopped		1

HARVEST MEAT:

½ cup very finely chopped lean pork	125 mL
1 cup very finely chopped boneless chicken breast	250 mL
2 egg yolks	2
1 tsp cornstarch	5 mL
Pinch each salt, sugar and freshly ground pepper	Pinch
1½ tsp light soy sauce	7 mL
1 tsp Oriental sesame oil	5 mL
½ tsp rice wine	2 mL

SNOW:

2½ oz rice noodles (vermicelli)	75 g
2 green onions, finely chopped	2
6 iceberg lettuce leaves, trimmed to form cups	6
Oil for deep-frying (about 6 cups/1.5 L)	

Mandarin harvest is a fragrant chicken, pork, mushroom and water chestnut mixture served over crispy, light-as-air rice vermicelli "snow."

HARVEST VEGETABLES: Soak dry mushrooms in warm water for 15 minutes. Discard stems and chop mushrooms finely. Arrange the onion, chestnuts and mushrooms in one bowl; measure out remaining harvest vegetable ingredients and set together by the stove.

HARVEST MEAT: In a bowl, combine ingredients for harvest meat and let stand at room temperature for 15 minutes.

SNOW: Separate strands of noodles to form a loose rectangle about 7 x 2 inches (17 x 5 cm). Heat a large wok over high heat. Add 3 cups (750 mL) oil and heat to 375°F (190°C). Pour about 2 inches (5 cm) oil into a deep fryer and heat over medium heat.

Cook harvest meat mixture in the wok, stirring all the time, until meat changes colour and becomes fluffy. Strain in sieve set over a bowl.

Drain all but 2 tbsp (25 mL) of oil from wok. Heat over high heat and add the onion, chestnuts and mushrooms and stir-fry. When you can "smell the good smell of onions," about 1 minute, add salt, soy sauce, rice wine and sesame oil. Return meat to wok and stir-fry for 2 to 3 minutes; remove from heat and stir in green onion.

While meat and vegetable "harvest" are cooking, increase heat under deep fryer until oil is 400°F (200°C). Drop a noodle into the oil to test its heat. Oil is ready when the noodle floats in 5 seconds and becomes fluffy. Drop the rice noodles into the oil. Count to 5 and turn over. Count to 5 and remove; drain noodles quickly on paper towels and set on a heated platter. Immediately pour meat and vegetable "harvest" over noodles, leaving 1-inch (2.5 cm) border. Garnish with green onions and bring to the table.

Cut the harvest in snow into individual portions and scoop up sauce and noodles in a lettuce cup.

Enough for 4 to 6, with other Chinese dishes.

Katie Williams' Devilishly Hot Barbecued Chicken

2	broiler/fryer chickens (2 to 3 lb/1 to 1.35 kg each)	2
⅓ cup	oil, preferably olive	75 mL
1 tbsp	white wine vinegar	15 mL
½ to 1 tsp	cayenne	2 to 5 mL
½ tsp	coarsely ground pepper	2 mL
2	large cloves garlic, minced	2
2 tbsp	finely chopped fresh parsley	25 mL
1 tsp	salt	5 mL
2	lemons	2

Katie and Roger Williams spend their summers at Lac Memphrémagog, Quebec, where they love to entertain. A few summers ago they fired up the outdoor barbecue and presented their guests with this Italian-inspired grilled chicken. Adjust the cayenne to suit your palate. Serve with marinated summer vegetables and a crusty bread.

Lay chickens on their breasts. Using kitchen shears, cut each one along both sides of the backbone and remove bone, including neck if it's attached. Snip off wings at the joint nearest the tip (reserve these bones for the stock pot). With a sharp heavy knife, split the breastbone lengthwise from inside the cavity. Trim off any excess skin. Place chickens skin side up and press down firmly on each breastbone, flattening the chicken as much as possible. Wipe and dry chickens thoroughly with paper towels.

Combine the oil, vinegar, cayenne, pepper, garlic and parsley in a large, sturdy plastic bag. Place chickens in the marinade and close with a twist tie. Let marinate for 2 hours at room temperature or up to 1 day in the refrigerator, turning chickens occasionally.

Place chickens skin side up on a greased rack about 4 inches (10 cm) from the coals and grill for 10 minutes. Salt lightly and turn over. Barbecue chicken skin side down until skin is crispy and well browned and the chicken is cooked through, about 8 minutes. To test for doneness, stick the tip of a pointed knife into the thigh and if juices run clear, the chicken is cooked. Baste the chicken as it grills with any remaining marinade. Salt skin side lightly and transfer to a heated platter.

Cut each lemon into 6 wedges and use to garnish chicken.

Makes 6 to 8 servings.

Chestnut Stuffing for Turkey

1 lb chestnuts	500 g
2 cups chicken stock (see page 60)	500 mL
¾ cup butter	175 mL
2 cups thinly sliced leeks (white and light green part only of 1 to 2 leeks)	500 mL
2 cups chopped celery (4 stalks)	500 mL
1 cup chopped onion (1 large)	250 mL
½ cup finely chopped carrot (1 large)	125 mL
4 tsp chopped fresh summer savory or marjoram or 2 tsp (10 mL) crumbled dried	20 mL
4 tsp chopped fresh sage or 2 tsp (10 mL) crumbled dried	20 mL
2 tsp salt	10 mL
½ tsp freshly ground pepper	2 mL
½ tsp chopped fresh thyme or ¼ tsp (1 mL) crumbled dried	2 mL
¼ tsp freshly grated nutmeg	1 mL
Pinch crushed rosemary	Pinch
1 tbsp grated orange peel	15 mL
⅓ cup orange juice	75 mL
12 cups slightly dry bread cubes	3 L

A good stuffing can only be made with good bread. It can be white or whole wheat but should not be sweetened. Let the loaf dry out for a day or two so the cubes will be firm, thus ensuring a light textured stuffing.

As for the chestnuts that make this stuffing special, enlist as many helpers as possible to peel them. The outside shells are easy to remove, but peeling the inner husks off a large quantity can be arduous for one person.

Rinse chestnuts under cold water. Cut a strip off the side of each one and boil for 5 minutes in water to cover. Using a slotted spoon, remove chestnuts from the water and peel off the outer shells and inner husks. If they become harder to peel as they cool, immerse them in hot water for a minute and proceed. Place peeled chestnuts in a clean saucepan (there should be about 2½ cups/625 mL). Cover with the stock and simmer, uncovered, for 30 to 40 minutes or until the chestnuts are translucent. Remove from the stock and set aside. Keep the stock for the turkey gravy.

Meanwhile, prepare the rest of the dressing. Melt butter in a large skillet. Add leeks, celery, onion, carrot, savory, sage, salt, pepper, thyme, nutmeg and rosemary. Cook gently for 20 minutes or until all the vegetables are translucent and the flavours have thoroughly blended. Add the chestnuts and fry for 5 minutes longer. Let cool and mix in the orange peel and juice.

Place the bread cubes in a large bowl and pour the vegetable mixture over. Toss gently but thoroughly to blend. Taste and add more salt if desired. Keep chilled until time to stuff and roast the bird. Never store a home-stuffed turkey, even in the freezer, before roasting.

There is enough delicious savoury dressing for a 14 to 16 pound (about 6.75 kg) turkey.

Along-the-Danforth Souvlakia

YOGURT SAUCE:

1½ cups natural yogurt		375 mL
1 large clove garlic, minced		1

MEAT AND MARINADE:

2 lb boned lean pork or lamb, in ¾-inch (2 cm) cubes		1 kg
4 tsp chopped fresh oregano or 2 tsp (10 mL) crumbled dried		20 mL
¼ tsp freshly ground pepper		1 mL
¼ cup lemon juice		50 mL

GRILLING AND SERVING:

¼ cup oil		50 mL
2 tsp chopped fresh oregano or 1 tsp (5 mL) crumbled dried		10 mL
Salt		
6 torpedo rolls		6
1 large tomato		1

From the Greek restaurants that line Danforth Avenue in Toronto, a new twist on souvlakia. In the old country, souvlakia was skewered tidbits of lamb, but here in Canada, tender lean pork often replaces the more expensive lamb. The herbs are the same and the yogurt sauce, courtesy of the Astoria Shish Kebab House, adds just the right amount of garlicky assertiveness. Torpedo rolls are long, crusty sesame buns.

YOGURT SAUCE: Wet a square of paper towel, wring out and use to line a colander or sieve. Place over a bowl and spoon in yogurt. Refrigerate and let the clear liquid drip out for about 6 hours. Stir the yogurt gently once or twice, being careful not to press it through the liner. When the yogurt is thick and its volume reduced by about half, transfer to a serving dish and mix in the garlic. Cover and refrigerate for up to 3 days.

MEAT AND MARINADE: Combine the meat and marinade ingredients in a plastic bag or glass bowl and close with a twist tie or cover. If using a bag, place in a bowl. Refrigerate for at least 2 hours or up to 1 day, turning as frequently as possible to flavour and tenderize the meat evenly.

GRILLING AND SERVING: To grill, remove meat from marinade. Drain and pat dry with paper towels. Thread onto 6 skewers, brush with oil and set on a rack about 4 inches (10 cm) from the heat. Grill or broil for 8 to 10 minutes, turning to brown pieces evenly. Adjust the distance from the heat if necessary to keep the meat sizzling but not burning. Remove from the grill and sprinkle with oregano and lightly with salt.

Split rolls lengthwise, leaving them hinged along one side. Toast rolls on the grill or under the broiler. Cut tomato in half from top to bottom and then into ¼-inch (5 mm)thick slices. Spread rolls generously with the yogurt sauce. Line one side of each roll with tomato slices. Slide the souvlakia off the skewers and arrange on the rolls. Press rolls together lightly and serve immediately.

Serves 6 copiously.

Tanya Sterioff's Ragout of Lamb with Spinach

3 lb lean boneless lamb, in 1½-inch (3 cm) cubes	1.35 kg
2 tbsp oil	25 mL
8 cups water	2 L
2 tbsp butter	25 mL
1 cup chopped green onions (4 large)	250 mL
1 fresh hot banana pepper, cored, seeded and chopped	1
1 tsp salt	5 mL
½ tsp freshly ground pepper	2 mL
½ tsp paprika	2 mL
1 cup chopped, peeled, seeded tomatoes	250 mL
1 cup long grain rice	250 mL
1 lb spinach	500 g

When Torontonian Tanya Sterioff came to my kitchen to show me some Macedonian cooking, she arrived early, and amid a whirlwind of roasting peppers, mashing feta cheese and chopping leeks, lamb and mint, we had a wonderful day. This stew was one of the highlights. Its beauty lies in the quality of the lamb — fresh Canadian lamb, preferably the shoulder.

In a large heavy saucepan over medium-high heat, brown the lamb on all sides in the oil. Add water, bring to a boil and cover partially. Reduce heat and simmer gently until tender, 45 minutes to 1 hour.

Meanwhile, in a skillet, melt butter. Sauté onions over medium heat for 5 minutes or until translucent. Add the pepper and sauté for 2 minutes. Mix in salt, pepper, paprika and tomatoes and fry gently for 8 minutes or until the ingredients begin to blend together.

Add sautéed vegetables to tender lamb. Rinse rice under cold water, add to stew and simmer, covered, for 5 minutes.

Wash spinach in 2 or 3 changes of lukewarm water. Shake off excess moisture and remove any blemishes and coarse stems. Add spinach to lamb and cook, covered, for about 10 minutes longer or until the rice is tender. Taste and adjust seasoning if desired.

Serve in heated bowls with an abundance of crusty bread to sop up the wonderful juices. A salad of full-flavored garden vegetables such as cucumbers, red and green bell peppers, tomatoes and sliced zucchini, redolent with garlic, ends the meal with a crunch.

Makes 6 servings.

Loin of Pork with Toasted Hazelnut Stuffing

½ cup hazelnuts	125 mL
¼ cup butter	50 mL
½ cup finely chopped onion (1 medium)	125 mL
½ cup finely chopped celery	125 mL
¼ cup finely chopped carrot	50 mL
1 clove garlic, minced	1
½ tsp salt	2 mL
½ tsp chopped fresh sage or ¼ tsp (1 mL) crumbled dried	2 mL
½ tsp chopped fresh thyme or ¼ tsp (1 mL) crumbled dried	2 mL
¼ tsp freshly ground pepper	1 mL
Pinch cloves	Pinch
1 cup stale but not dry bread crumbs	250 mL
⅓ cup raisins	75 mL
6 lb loin of pork, either centre cut or centre to tenderloin	2.75 kg
1 tbsp Dijon mustard	15 mL
1 tbsp flour	15 mL
1½ cups (approx) water	375 mL
¼ cup dry white vermouth	50 mL

Ask your butcher to cut the backbone to separate the chops. You can then extend the cuts into the meat to form pockets just large enough to accommodate a tablespoon (15 mL) or so of this nutty stuffing. This dish is elegant enough for fall or winter entertaining.

Toast hazelnuts in a single layer at 325°F (160°C) for 10 minutes or until skins crack and the flesh is golden. Rub vigorously in a terry kitchen cloth to remove most of the skins. Chop nuts finely and transfer to a large bowl.

In a medium skillet, melt butter over moderate heat. Add onion, celery, carrot and garlic; cook until tender, about 5 minutes. Stir in salt, sage, thyme, pepper and cloves. Add to nuts; stir in bread crumbs and raisins and toss together.

Wipe meat with a damp cloth and extend pockets between chops if necessary. Place about 1 tbsp (15 mL) stuffing in each pocket. Tie loin from end to end with kitchen string; place fat side up on a rack in roasting pan. Brush roast with a thin coating of mustard and season with salt and pepper.

Roast, uncovered, at 325°F (160°C) until meat thermometer registers 170°F (75°C), about 30 minutes per pound (500 g). At this temperature, the meat is done but still juicy.

Remove meat from oven and transfer to a heated platter. Cover lightly and let stand for 10 minutes before carving. Remove string.

Meanwhile, skim fat from meat juices in roasting pan. Combine flour, water and vermouth and pour into pan. Cook over high heat, stirring up brown bits from bottom of the pan. Add more water if necessary for gravy. Season with salt and pepper and serve in a heated sauce boat.

Carve loin into chops, including a portion of stuffing with each serving. Pass the gravy separately.

Makes 8 generous servings.

Tourtière Tarts

2 lb ground lean pork	1 kg
1½ cups finely chopped onions (2 medium)	375 mL
1 large clove garlic, minced	1
4 tsp chopped fresh sage or 2 tsp (10 mL) crumbled dried	20 mL
2 tsp salt	10 mL
½ tsp celery seed	2 mL
½ tsp freshly ground pepper	2 mL
¼ tsp cloves	1 mL
½ cup water	125 mL
2 cups finely riced or mashed potatoes (3 medium, boiled)	500 mL
Pastry for 26 double-crust tarts (equivalent of 4 single-crust pies)	

In the last decade or two, tourtière pie has jumped the Quebec border and become Christmas fare across the country. This version of the crusty little tarts is ideal for hors d'oeuvre and can be made ahead and frozen. Serve with spicy hot chili sauce, page 139.

In a large saucepan, combine pork, onions, garlic, sage, salt, celery seed, pepper, cloves and water. Bring to a boil and cook, uncovered, stirring to break up meat until meat loses its red color and about half the moisture has evaporated.

Cover, reduce heat and simmer for 45 minutes. Let cool to room temperature, then tip pan and skim off excess fat. Blend in mashed potatoes; taste and adjust seasoning.

Line twenty-six 3-inch (7 cm) tart tins with pastry. Fill with pork mixture, mounding if necessary, and cover with a round of pastry cut to fit just inside top of tart. Prick a small steam hole in the covering pastry. Freeze at this stage if desired.

Bake at 425°F (220°C) for 20 to 25 minutes or until pastry has browned and the filling is bubbly. Serve hot.

Makes 26 snack-sized tourtières.

Chops with Winter Dried Fruit

6 pork chops, about 3/4 inch (2 cm) thick (2 lb/1 kg total)	6
1 tbsp oil	15 mL
3/4 tsp salt	4 mL
1/4 tsp freshly ground pepper	1 mL
1/4 tsp cinnamon	1 mL
Pinch allspice	Pinch
1/2 tsp Worcestershire sauce	2 mL
1 tsp grated orange peel	5 mL
2 cups orange juice	500 mL
1 1/2 cups mixed dried fruit (apricots, pitted prunes, apples and pears)	375 mL
1/4 cup raisins	50 mL
2 tsp cornstarch	10 mL
2 tbsp water	25 mL

The next time you pick up a package of pork chops, think of them nestled in this orange fruit sauce, and pick up the other ingredients too. Choose loin chops if the budget permits or the darker, fuller flavoured shoulder or butt chops.

Trim excess fat from chops and nick edges to keep them from curling while cooking. In a large skillet, heat oil over medium-high heat and brown chops on both sides. Drain fat.

Sprinkle chops evenly with salt, pepper, cinnamon, allspice, Worcestershire and orange peel. Pour 1 cup (250 mL) of the juice over the chops and cover with a tightly fitting lid. Simmer over low heat for 45 minutes. Turn chops.

Chop fruit coarsely and strew fruit and raisins over meat. Pour in the rest of the juice and simmer, covered, until chops are tender and the fruit plump, about 20 minutes.

Remove chops to a heated platter and keep warm. Mix together cornstarch and water; stir into sauce and cook, stirring, for 2 to 3 minutes over medium-high heat until sauce thickens slightly and clears. Pour over chops and serve immediately.

Makes 6 servings.

Sautéed Rabbit with Prunes and Red Wine

1 rabbit (about 3 lb/ 1.35 kg)		1
¼ lb prunes		125 g
1 cup water		250 mL
¼ cup flour		50 mL
2 tbsp each butter and oil		25 mL
1 cup finely chopped onions		250 mL
1 tsp salt		5 mL
¼ tsp freshly ground pepper		1 mL
⅓ cup dry red wine		75 mL
6 strips orange peel		6

MARINADE:

1 cup dry red wine	250 mL
2 tbsp red wine vinegar	25 mL
1 strip orange peel	1
5 each whole pepper-corns, cracked, and juniper berries	5
2 sprigs fresh thyme or ½ tsp (2 mL) crumbled dried	2
2 whole cloves	2
1 bay leaf	1
4 sprigs fresh parsley	4
½ cup finely chopped onion	125 mL

Of all game, rabbit may be the easiest to buy in butcher shops and supermarkets. Marinate with orange peel, wine, juniper berries and cloves to make a zesty dinner party dish. Serve with steamed green beans or snow peas, or zucchini slices sautéed in butter with rosemary.

Remove head from rabbit and cut rabbit into 6 pieces.

MARINADE: Combine all ingredients for marinade in a large sturdy plastic bag (a large freezer bag is excellent). Place bag in shallow dish.

Place rabbit pieces in the bag of marinade, close the top firmly with a twist tie and lay flat in the dish. Marinate rabbit for 2 to 4 hours in the refrigerator, turning the bag periodically.

Soak prunes in water until plump and tender; soft prunes may need as little as 1 hour while hard dry prunes may need to soak several hours.

Remove rabbit from marinade and wipe dry. Toss rabbit in the flour and reserve on paper towels. Strain the marinade, pressing out and reserving all liquid but discarding the flavouring ingredients.

In a large heavy saucepan, melt the butter. Add oil and brown the rabbit on all sides over medium-high heat. Remove rabbit and reserve. Sauté onions in the pan for 5 minutes. Return rabbit to pan and add the salt, pepper, wine, strained marinade, prunes and their soaking water. Mix gently but thoroughly to blend all the ingredients. Bring to a boil, then reduce heat and simmer, partially covered, for 30 to 40 minutes or until rabbit is tender and the sauce thickened.

Taste and adjust seasoning if desired. Transfer to a heated serving platter and garnish with orange peel.

Makes 6 servings.

Cheddar Cheese Soufflé

1/4 cup butter	50 mL
1/4 cup flour	50 mL
1 tsp salt	5 mL
Pinch each cayenne, freshly ground pepper and nutmeg	Pinch
1 1/4 cups hot milk	300 mL
5 egg yolks	5
6 egg whites	6
Pinch cream of tartar	Pinch
1 1/4 cups grated old Cheddar cheese (5 oz/150 g)	300 mL

Old Cheddar, especially when made with raw milk, has plenty of nip for a soufflé. Although you might not think of them as "Canadian," soufflés have appeared in our cookbooks since the turn of the century, under the name of "fondues."

In a heavy saucepan, melt butter; stir in flour, salt and spices and cook for 2 to 3 minutes, stirring constantly and without letting the roux brown.

Gradually whisk in milk to make a smooth sauce. Cook, uncovered, over low heat for 5 minutes, stirring frequently. Remove from heat and beat in egg yolks, one at a time.

In a large bowl, beat egg whites at low speed until frothy; add cream of tartar and beat at high speed until firm moist peaks form. Stir about 1/4 of the whites into the sauce. Scrape this lightened sauce over remaining whites and sprinkle with 1 cup (250 mL) of the cheese. Fold together smoothly.

Transfer to a greased 6-cup (1.5 L) soufflé dish and bake in the centre of an oven preheated to 375°F (190°C) for 35 to 40 minutes or until puffy and golden. To test for doneness, jiggle the dish gently; if the soufflé wobbles in the middle, bake for 5 minutes longer and test again.

Serve immediately with a green salad or sliced tomatoes dressed with a basil vinaigrette.

Serves 4 to 6, depending on size of eaters and other components of the meal.

Charcoal Barbecued Whitefish

1 whitefish, about $2\frac{1}{4}$ lb (1 kg)	1
1 cup loosely packed fresh whole herbs such as parsley, tarragon, thyme or summer savory	250 mL
3 tbsp oil	50 mL
2 tbsp dry white wine or vermouth	25 mL
$1\frac{1}{2}$ tbsp finely chopped fresh herbs, the same as above	20 mL
$\frac{1}{4}$ tsp freshly ground pepper	1 mL
Salt	
1 lemon	1

The Canadian tradition of cooking game and fish over the coals goes back a long way. West Coast Indians specialized in barbecued fish, and used a spit or grill made from green wood to hold their catch. A modern fish-shaped wire basket, available in kitchen stores, holds fish securely and allows the cook to grill both sides.

Whitefish is an excellent choice for barbecuing. Its skin becomes crisp and tasty, and its flesh moist. It marries beautifully with fresh herbs. But you'll also get good results if you use this recipe and technique to grill other fish about this size such as lake trout, pickerel, salmon trout and small whole salmon.

Clean and scale fish, or have the fishmonger do it. Wipe inside and out with a damp cloth. Cut 4 diagonal slashes about $\frac{1}{4}$ inch (5 mm) deep, about 3 inches (7 cm) long and about 2 inches (5 cm) apart along each side of the fish. These slashes allow the marinade to penetrate the fish.

Stuff whole herbs into fish cavity. Combine oil, wine, chopped herbs and pepper in a shallow glass dish. Lay fish in the marinade and turn to coat both sides. Cover and marinate for 2 hours in the refrigerator, turning the fish 2 or 3 times.

Place fish in the bottom half of a lightly oiled grilling basket. Clamp the top in place. Stand the grilling basket on its legs in the centre of the barbecue, banking coals up around the thickest part of the fish. Grill, calculating 10 minutes cooking time for every 1 inch (2.5 cm) of thickness of fish. Turn fish halfway through allotted time. Brush any remaining marinade over fish as it grills. Begin testing for doneness before the time is up and remove fish from grill as soon as flesh becomes opaque and flakes easily near the bone. If the thinner tail section is cooked before the mid-section, move coals away from that area.

Salt fish lightly on both sides. Transfer to a warm platter. Cut lemon into sixths lengthwise; remove seeds and arrange around fish.

Makes 4 generous servings. Increase number of fish for a large group of family and friends.

Poached Sole and Smoked Salmon Rolls

4 fillets of sole (4 to 6 oz/ 125 to 175 g each)		4
Salt and freshly ground pepper		
4 large or 8 small thin slices smoked salmon		4
1 tbsp butter, softened		15 mL
⅓ cup finely chopped tender celery		75 mL
¼ cup finely chopped leek, white part only		50 mL
¼ cup finely chopped carrot		50 mL
2 tbsp finely chopped shallot		25 mL
⅔ cup dry white wine		150 mL
½ cup fish stock (see page 44) or clam juice		125 mL
3 tbsp dry white vermouth		50 mL
1¼ cups whipping cream		300 mL
1 tsp each soft butter and flour (optional)		5 mL

From the repertoire of Ian Neilson, a winner in the Culinary Olympics and catalyst among Calgary chefs and cooking students, here is a perfect entrée for a dinner party. White sole rolled with pink smoked salmon fillets pleases the eye, and doubly pleases the palate.

Flatten fillets of sole slightly with flat side of a cleaver. Season on both sides with salt and pepper.

Lay 1 or 2 slices of smoked salmon on top of each fillet. Starting at wide end, roll up salmon and sole. Fasten firmly with toothpicks.

Use 1 tbsp (15 mL) of butter to grease a shallow heatproof pan large enough to hold all the rolls side by side. Sprinkle celery, leek, carrot and shallot over buttered pan. Set rolls, seam side down, on the bed of vegetables. Drizzle with wine, stock and vermouth. Cover with buttered waxed paper and foil. Bring to a boil over high heat on the top of the stove. Immediately pop into oven preheated to 350°F (180°C) and poach until fish rolls are opaque and flaky, 10 to 15 minutes.

Remove rolls from pan, picking off any of the flavoring vegetables that may have stuck to them. Gently pull out toothpicks and keep rolls warm in a heated serving dish.

Boil poaching liquid over high heat for 4 minutes. Strain into a medium saucepan, pressing all juices from vegetables. Add any juices that may have accumulated around fish rolls and the cream. Mix together butter and flour if using and blend into sauce. Bring to a full boil and boil hard for 3 to 4 minutes or until sauce is thick enough to coat a spoon lightly. Taste and adjust seasoning.

Spoon sauce over fish rolls. Serve with steamed sugar snap or snow peas, freshly shelled garden peas, fresh asparagus or spinach.

Makes 4 servings.

Poached Halibut with Beurre Blanc

2 tbsp butter	25 mL
½ cup each chopped carrot, onion and celery	125 mL
1 tsp salt	5 mL
3 peppercorns, crushed	3
4 sprigs fresh parsley	4
1 sprig each fresh thyme and tarragon or ½ tsp (2 mL) crumbled dried	1
1 bay leaf	1
5 cups water	1.25 L
1 lb fish scraps and bones	500 g
2 lb halibut steaks or fillets, about 1 inch (2.5 cm) thick	1 kg
Chopped fresh parsley, chervil or watercress	

BEURRE BLANC:

1 tsp finely chopped shallot or onion	5 mL
⅓ cup dry white wine	75 mL
2 tbsp white wine vinegar	25 mL
1 tbsp whipping cream	15 mL
5 tbsp unsalted butter	75 mL
Pinch salt	Pinch

A piece of perfectly poached halibut with buttery sauce, enjoyed at the Captain's House in Chester, Nova Scotia, inspired this dish.

In a large saucepan or stock pot, melt butter. Add vegetables, cover and cook gently for 5 minutes, stirring once or twice. Add salt, peppercorns, parsley, thyme, tarragon, bay leaf, water and fish scraps and bring to a boil over high heat. Skim off scum, reduce heat and simmer for 30 minutes. Strain, discarding the flavouring vegetables and fish scraps. This fish stock can be used immediately or kept in the refrigerator for a few days or up to 3 months in the freezer.

To poach halibut, pour strained stock into a large shallow saucepan. Bring to a boil. Add fish in single layer and bring stock back to a boil. Reduce heat so liquid bubbles gently. Time the fish, allowing 10 minutes for every 1 inch (2.5 cm) thickness at the thickest point or until fish is opaque and flakes easily. Immediately lift out with a wide spatula and drain on paper towels. (You can cool and freeze stock for another use.) Remove skin and arrange fish on a warmed serving platter. Garnish with parsley.

BEURRE BLANC: Meanwhile, combine shallot, wine and vinegar in a small saucepan. Simmer over medium heat until liquid is reduced to about 2 tbsp (25 mL). Strain and stir in cream. Cut butter into 15 pieces. Bring sauce back to a boil and immediately turn heat down to its lowest setting. Whisk in butter, 1 piece at a time. Taste and season with salt. Serve immediately in a warmed sauceboat.

Makes 6 servings.

Granville Island Market Whole Baked Salmon with Wild Rice

1 cup wild rice (6 oz/175 g)	250 mL
2 cups water	500 mL
1 tsp salt	5 mL
2 tbsp butter	25 mL
1 cup finely chopped mushrooms (4 oz/125 g)	250 mL
½ cup finely chopped onion (1 medium)	125 mL
1 clove garlic, minced	1
½ cup slivered almonds or pine nuts	125 mL
2 tsp chopped fresh thyme or 1 tsp (5 mL) crumbled dried	10 mL
1 tsp chopped fresh sage or ½ tsp (2 mL) crumbled dried	5 mL
¼ tsp freshly ground pepper	1 mL
2 tbsp lemon juice	25 mL
4 to 5 lb fresh whole salmon	2 kg
1 tbsp melted butter	15 mL

GARNISH:

Watercress	
2 lemons, cut into wedges	2

From lively Granville Market on Vancouver's waterfront comes a recipe that combines two of Canada's most aristocratic products.

Rinse rice and place in a saucepan with water and half the salt. Cover and bring to a boil. Reduce heat and simmer until rice is tender, but not mushy, 25 to 30 minutes. Uncover and cook briefly if any moisture remains. Spread rice on a tray to cool.

Meanwhile, in a large skillet, melt butter. Sauté mushrooms, onion, garlic, almonds, thyme, sage, pinch of salt and pepper until vegetables are tender and nuts slightly browned. Combine with rice and 1 tbsp (15 mL) of the lemon juice. Taste and add more seasoning if desired.

Wipe salmon cavity and exterior with a damp cloth. Brush cavity with remaining lemon juice and salt and fill with stuffing. Place any leftover stuffing in a heatproof dish and cover. Sew, or skewer and lace the cavity closed.

Place fish on a lightly greased baking pan and brush with butter. Measure fish at the thickest point, including stuffing, and bake at 450°F (230°C) for 10 minutes for every 1 inch (2.5 cm) thickness. Bake any extra stuffing along with the fish. Let fish rest for 5 minutes in a warm spot. Transfer to a heated platter and carefully remove string and skin from the top side of salmon. Garnish with watercress and lemon wedges. Arrange extra stuffing around cavity opening.

Makes 8 to 10 servings. Spring vegetables, such as asparagus or fiddleheads, with a hollandaise sauce make splendid accompaniments.

Barbecued Salmon Steaks

$\frac{1}{4}$ cup chopped fresh dill	50 mL
2 tsp grated lemon peel	10 mL
$\frac{1}{3}$ cup oil	75 mL
6 salmon steaks, $1\frac{1}{4}$ inches (3 cm) thick ($\frac{1}{2}$ lb/250 g each)	6
Salt and freshly ground pepper	
2 lemons, cut into wedges	2

The firm flesh, distinctive peach colour and rich flavour of red spring salmon make it an ideal choice for the barbecue or hibachi. (But all Pacific or Atlantic salmon, and even halibut or cod steaks, make excellent barbecue fare.)

Salmon steaks must be at least 1 inch (2.5 cm) thick so they won't dry out over the coals. The rule of thumb for cooking is 10 minutes for every 1 inch (2.5 cm) of thickness, cooked 4 inches (10 cm) from the coals.

Combine dill, lemon peel and oil in a flat glass or enamel dish large enough to accommodate the steaks in single layer. Add the steaks and turn to coat both sides with the marinade. Cover and refrigerate for 2 to 8 hours.

Brush barbecue grill with oil and position about 4 inches (10 cm) above coals. Using a long wide spatula, place steaks on the grill and grill for 5 minutes. Turn carefully and grill for 7 to 8 minutes on the other side, brushing periodically with any remaining marinade. Salmon is done when fish flakes easily from the bone.

Season lightly with salt and pepper and serve with lemon wedges.

Makes 6 generous servings.

Butter Barbecued Scallops

2 lb large scallops	1 kg
$\frac{1}{2}$ tsp salt	2 mL
$\frac{1}{4}$ tsp freshly ground pepper	1 mL
$\frac{1}{2}$ cup butter, melted	125 mL
1 cup fine, stale but not dry bread crumbs	250 mL

Summer cooking is easy when all the chef has to do is barbecue a pound or two of scallops. Serve with a green summer vegetable — skinny green beans can't be beat — and a cucumber and tomato salad.

Pat scallops thoroughly dry and season evenly with salt and pepper. Dip in melted butter and roll in crumbs. If preparing an hour to two in advance, place the scallops on a tray, cover lightly and refrigerate.

Thread scallops onto 6 to 8 skewers, spacing scallops

close but not touching, or place on a greased wire grill.

Barbecue on a greased grill about 4 inches (10 cm) from the coals for 8 to 12 minutes, depending on size, turning scallops as they cook to brown crumbs evenly.

Serve immediately to 6 to 8 lucky eaters.

Note: As a variation on this recipe, substitute 1 lb (500 g) filleted salmon for half the scallops. Cut into cubes the same size as the scallops and alternate on the skewers.

Oaten Trout

When Dennis and Joanne Cole invite friends to stay in their Thornbury, Ontario, chalet for a weekend of skiing, they often serve fresh trout. Luckily their chalet is close to Aquafarms, an impressive trout farm where buyers can select their own fish. Dennis uses the Aquafarms recipe, adapted below, to produce a succulent pan-fried trout in a crisp, almost nutty, rolled oats coating. Cleaned, individual portion-sized trout are available in many fishmongers; some even have a tank so you can choose your own supper. Anglers can, of course, go from creel to frying pan.

4 cleaned trout, (8 to 12 oz/250 to 375 g each)	4
2 tbsp flour	25 mL
½ tsp salt	2 mL
¼ tsp freshly ground pepper	1 mL
1 egg	1
1½ cups regular rolled oats	375 mL
¼ cup butter	50 mL

GARNISH:

1 lemon, cut into wedges	1
Watercress	

Rinse and pat trout dry. Measure at the thickest part of the back. Combine flour, salt and pepper in a paper bag. Shake trout, one at a time, in seasoned flour.

Beat egg; pour into a shallow narrow dish. Spread 1 cup (250 mL) of the oats in a similar dish and sprinkle remainder on a tray large enough to hold trout in single layer. Dip each trout in the egg, then in the rolled oats, coating both sides. Set on oat-sprinkled tray. Trout can be covered loosely and refrigerated for up to 2 hours before cooking.

Melt butter in a large skillet over medium-high heat. Fry trout until crisp and golden brown on both sides, calculating about 10 minutes cooking time for every 1 inch (2.5 cm) thickness of trout.

Transfer to heated dinner plates and garnish with lemon and watercress. Makes 4 moderate-to-generous servings, depending on size of trout.

Mussels in White Wine

5 lb mussels	2.25 kg
$\frac{1}{3}$ cup butter	75 mL
$\frac{2}{3}$ cup finely chopped shallots or onion (4 shallots or 1 onion)	150 mL
$\frac{1}{3}$ cup finely chopped carrot (1 small)	75 mL
$\frac{1}{4}$ cup finely chopped tender celery	50 mL
1 bay leaf	1
4 stalks parsley	4
1 sprig fresh thyme or pinch crumbled dried	1
Pinch freshly ground pepper	Pinch
$2\frac{1}{2}$ cups dry white wine	625 mL
$\frac{1}{3}$ cup finely chopped fresh parsley	75 mL
1 tbsp finely chopped fresh tarragon or $1\frac{1}{2}$ tsp (7 mL) crumbled dried	15 mL

Mussels make an ideal dish when friends drop over — quick to prepare, fun and informal to eat. Eating mussels in white wine is an "all fingers" operation. Bend off one half of the shell and bite off the succulent peach-coloured meat. Use the now-empty half shell to scoop up some of the broth. A fair amount of slurping is bound to occur. An accomplished mussel-eater finishes mussels and broth simultaneously.

Scrub mussels in cold water using a brush or nylon scouring square. With a paring knife, pull out and cut off beard-like string that sticks out from the shells. Keep mussels covered and chilled while preparing sauce. Prepare the mussels just before cooking to keep the mortality rate low.

In a large heavy saucepan, melt butter and cook shallots, carrot and celery over moderate heat for 5 minutes. With a piece of string, tie together bay leaf, parsley stalks and thyme; add to pan along with pepper and wine. Bring to a boil. Reduce heat and simmer, uncovered, for 5 minutes.

Add mussels all at once. Cover, increase heat to medium-high and cook for 5 to 8 minutes, shaking the saucepan vigorously 2 or 3 times while the mussels steam. Uncover and discard any mussels that remain closed. Discard the bundle of herbs.

Distribute mussels evenly among 6 large warmed shallow soup or pasta bowls. Add chopped parsley and tarragon to the broth and pour over mussels. Serve immediately.

Makes 6 servings. Put out a loaf or two of crusty bread for sopping up the juices.

VEGETABLES

Frankly, while I feel sorry for people who don't like vegetables, I secretly think that it leaves all the more for me. I can't remember a time when vegetables weren't a treat — but then I grew up enjoying my mother and father's homegrown produce. What we didn't grow in the lovingly tended garden behind the house, we got from the Stratford market. Our family feasted in the spring on asparagus and the first lettuces coaxed out of a sunny protected corner of the garden. Summer brought skinny beans, baby beets and juicy ripe tomatoes to our table, followed by our own carrots, cabbages, onions and acorn squash in the fall and winter. They're now in their mid-seventies but my parents, Frank and Olive Davis, are still keen gardeners. They eat their fill all summer, preserve plenty for the winter and happily supply friends, neighbours and lucky family members like myself with everything from garden cress and sugar snap peas to kohlrabi and tomatoes — especially tomatoes.

I think it's this love of gardening that gave our family its passion for salads and well-cooked vegetables. We knew what fresh vegetables tasted like and it was simply unthinkable to ruin their delicate tastes by overcooking. After all, hadn't we brought them to life from seed, watered and hoed them, and plucked them at their prime?

The appreciation of simply prepared vegetables spans over 100 years from Mrs. Nourse's 1845 recipe for "spinage" to a 1980s recipe for spaghetti squash. My other favourites go beyond the boil-and-butter approach with savoury medleys of vegetables, such as leeks and tomatoes and the barbecued zucchini and cherry tomatoes. Sample some of the cuisines that make Canadian cooking so rich and varied — Mennonite schmoor kohl, the Carlino garlic artichokes and the stir-fried broccoli and red peppers.

Barbecued Cherry Tomatoes and Zucchini

4 small zucchini (1 lb/500 g total)	4
12 cherry tomatoes	12

MARINADE:

3 tbsp olive oil	50 mL
1 tbsp lemon juice	15 mL
1 tbsp chopped green onion or chives	15 mL
1 tsp chopped fresh marjoram, thyme or oregano or ½ tsp (2 mL) crumbled dried	5 mL
¼ tsp freshly ground pepper	1 mL
Salt	

Summer cooks have discovered that not only meat and fish are enhanced by barbecuing. Vegetables can sizzle over the coals too and, in winter, cook under the grill. Serve this tomato-zucchini combination on a bed of rice with roast lamb, grilled chicken or fish.

Wash zucchini thoroughly; trim stem and blossom ends and score zucchini lengthwise in 5 places. Drop into a pan of boiling water and blanch for 3 minutes. Remove and immediately drop into cold water to stop cooking. Drain, pat dry and cut into 1-inch (2.5 cm) lengths. Remove stems from tomatoes; rinse and dry.

MARINADE: Combine all ingredients except the salt in a shallow dish. Add the vegetables and toss gently until thoroughly coated. Cover and marinate for 1 hour at room temperature or up to 4 hours in the refrigerator, stirring periodically.

Thread vegetables onto 6 skewers, starting with a chunk of zucchini, and using 3 zucchini chunks and 2 tomatoes per skewer.

Grill about 6 inches (15 cm) from the heat for 2 minutes. Turn, brush with any remaining marinade for 2 minutes longer or until vegetables are tender inside and slightly crispy and charred outside. Sprinkle lightly with salt and serve.

Makes 6 servings.

Dressed "Spinage"

1 lb spinach	500 g
3 tbsp butter	50 mL
¼ cup whipping cream	50 mL

From *Modern Cookery*, written by a Mrs. Nourse and published in Montreal by Armour & Ramsay in 1845, here is a recipe that presents "spinage" at its simple best. The quotations are from Mrs. Nourse.

Pinch freshly grated nutmeg	Pinch
Salt	

Wash spinach in 2 or 3 changes of lukewarm water. Trim off coarse stems and blemishes. Drain and shake.

Place the spinach with "the water that hangs about it" in a large heavy saucepan. Cover and cook over medium-high heat for 3 minutes. Uncover, turn the spinach with a fork and continue cooking, covered, for 2 to 3 minutes or just until wilted.

Drain in a colander, pressing out excess juices. Now, according to Mrs. Nourse, the "spinage" should be "a fine green." Transfer to a board and chop finely or coarsely according to your taste.

In a skillet, melt the butter. Mix in the spinach, cream, nutmeg and salt and "when hot, dish it up."

Makes 3 or 4 servings. Excellent with fish, chicken or veal.

Green Corn Pudding

4 eggs	4
¾ cup light cream	175 mL
2 tbsp finely chopped fresh chives or green onions	25 mL
1 tbsp finely chopped fresh parsley	15 mL
½ tsp salt	2 mL
Pinch each freshly ground black pepper and cayenne	Pinch
2 cups corn kernels (3 to 4 cobs)	500 mL
½ cup grated old Cheddar cheese (white preferred)	125 mL
¾ cup fine but not dry bread crumbs	175 mL
2 tbsp butter, melted	25 mL
Boiling water	

"Green corn" is what fresh corn used to be called to distinguish it from the dry kernels that were available all year. Green corn pudding is a savoury custard that came to Canada with the Loyalists.

In a large bowl, beat together eggs and cream. Mix in the chives, parsley, salt, pepper, cayenne, corn and cheese. Measure out ¼ cup (50 mL) of the bread crumbs; combine with the butter and reserve. Mix the remaining crumbs into the corn custard.

Transfer custard to a well buttered 8-inch square (2 L) ovenproof dish (a cake pan works well). Place the dish in a larger shallow pan; pour enough boiling water into the outer pan to come ⅔ up the sides of the custard dish. Bake at 350°F (180°C) for 25 to 30 minutes or until a skewer inserted in the middle comes out clean. Remove the custard dish from the pan. Sprinkle the buttered crumbs over the surface and set on a rack 4 inches (10 cm) from the broiler. Broil for 2 to 3 minutes to brown the crumbs. Cut into squares and serve immediately.

Makes 6 servings.

Sherried Onions

6 medium-large onions (1½ lb/750 g)	6
¼ cup butter	50 mL
¼ cup dry sherry	50 mL
½ tsp salt	2 mL
¼ tsp ground coriander	1 mL
Pinch freshly ground pepper	Pinch

Onions simmered slowly in butter and sherry develop a wonderful rich flavour and a golden caramel colour. They add an inexpensive but elegant touch to a roast of beef, lamb or pork, as well as roast chicken or game poultry. In the fall, substitute whole pearl onions for the bigger halved onions; cut a shallow "x" in root end of each onion to keep them whole.

Peel onions; cut in half from stem to root end. In a large saucepan or skillet, melt butter over medium heat. Add onions in one layer cut side down and cook until cut side is butterscotch brown, 4 to 5 minutes. Turn over and gently fry rounded side for 4 to 5 minutes. Don't worry about browning the whole rounded half.

Drizzle sherry over cut side of each onion and sprinkle with salt, coriander and pepper. Cover and cook over very low heat for 1 to 1½ hours, basting the onions every 10 minutes or so with pan juices until browned and glazed.

Transfer onions carefully with a slotted spoon to a warmed serving dish or arrange around roast.

Makes 6 servings of 2 half onions each.

Schmoor Kohl

6 cups firmly packed sliced cabbage	1.5 L
1 cup chopped dried apples	250 mL
7 large unpitted prunes	7
⅓ cup water	75 mL
3 tbsp oil	50 mL
3 tbsp granulated sugar	50 mL
1 tsp salt	5 mL

Naturally dried apples, which Mennonite families still make every fall, are darker brown than the commercially dried fruit, and worth seeking out for their flavour. Schmoor kohl, a Mennonite dish of cabbage simmered with apples and prunes, is also a superior way to serve cabbage.

Place all the ingredients in a large heavy saucepan and mix well. Cover tightly and bring to a simmer over medium heat. Adjust the heat so the schmoor kohl cooks gently, stirring occasionally, for 1 to 1½ hours or until tender and well blended. Taste and add more salt if desired.

Makes 6 servings.

Stir-fried Broccoli and Red Peppers

1 tbsp sesame seeds	15 mL
1 bunch broccoli (1½ lb/750 g)	1
½ cup boiling chicken stock	125 mL
2 tsp cornstarch	10 mL
1 tsp light soy sauce	5 mL
½ tsp salt	2 mL
2 tbsp vegetable oil	25 mL
2 large cloves garlic, minced	2
1 tsp finely chopped fresh ginger	5 mL
1 large onion, sliced	1
1 large sweet red bell pepper (8 oz/250 g), seeded and sliced	1
8 oz small mushrooms	250 g
1 tsp Oriental sesame oil	5 mL

A colourful wok full of vegetables to go with Chinese dishes, chicken or fish.

In a small dry skillet, toast sesame seeds over medium heat, stirring frequently, for 8 to 10 minutes or until golden brown. Set aside for garnishing.

Trim broccoli and thinly peel stalks. Cut into bite-sized pieces. In a large saucepan, simmer broccoli in boiling stock until barely tender, 2 to 3 minutes. Remove broccoli and set aside. Measure out ⅓ cup (75 mL) of the stock and let cool; mix with the cornstarch, soy sauce and salt and set in a dish by the stove.

Heat a large wok over high heat. Add vegetable oil and heat until a drop of water sizzles in the oil. Stir in garlic and ginger and fry, stirring constantly, for 30 seconds. Remove garlic and ginger with a slotted spoon and discard.

Add onion and red pepper; stir-fry for 1 minute. Add mushrooms and stir-fry for 2 minutes. Add broccoli and stir-fry just until heated through.

Stir the cornstarch mixture and pour over vegetables. Cook for 30 seconds, stirring constantly to coat vegetables evenly. When vegetables glisten and sauce has thickened, drizzle with sesame oil. Transfer to a heated platter and sprinkle with toasted sesame seeds.

Makes 6 servings.

Lenore Barrett's Potato Latkes

6 medium potatoes (2 lb/1 kg total)	6
1 tbsp finely chopped onion	15 mL
2 eggs	2
2 tbsp matzo meal or all-purpose flour	25 mL
½ tsp salt	2 mL
¼ tsp baking powder	1 mL
½ cup (approx) oil	125 mL
1 cup sour cream (optional)	250 mL
2 cups applesauce (optional)	500 mL

When Toronto cooking school teacher Lucille Lorie gave me her daughter Lenore's recipe for Hanukkah latkes, she revealed her three secrets for making crisp and tasty potato pancakes. First, soak the grated potatoes in cold water overnight in the refrigerator; second, press all the water out of the soaked potatoes. The third secret is to add a touch of baking powder to the batter just before frying.

Grate potatoes on a medium grater or with the grating blade of a food processor. Place in a bowl, cover with cold water and let stand overnight in the refrigerator.

Drain potatoes in a colander, pressing and squeezing the potatoes dry with your hands. In a large bowl, combine potatoes, onion, eggs, matzo meal, salt and baking powder. Mix until well blended.

In a large skillet, heat 2 tbsp (25 mL) of the oil until hot. Take a tablespoon (15 mL) of latke mixture and place in pan, patting it thin and flat. You should be able to get 6 latkes into the pan. Fry over medium-high heat until latkes are very crisp and the edges are brown. Turn and brown other side. Regulate the heat so latkes sizzle without burning.

Drain latkes on paper towels and serve immediately with sour cream and/or apple sauce. Continue frying remaining batter, adding more oil to keep pan greased. Although latkes are at their best right from the pan, they can be reheated in a single layer on a baking sheet at 400°F (200°C) for 5 minutes.

Makes enough for 6 servings.

Mushroom and Barley Pilaf

1/3 cup butter	75 mL	
1/2 cup slivered or chopped unblanched almonds	125 mL	
1 cup chopped onions (2 medium)	250 mL	
1 cup chopped celery (2 stalks)	250 mL	
3 cups sliced button mushrooms (1/2 lb/250 g)	750 mL	
2 cups pot barley (14 oz/400 g)	500 mL	
4 cups hot chicken stock (see page 60)	1 L	
1 tsp salt	5 mL	
1/4 tsp freshly ground pepper	1 mL	
1 bay leaf	1	
1/4 tsp crushed dried thyme	1 mL	
1/4 cup chopped fresh dill	50 mL	
1/4 cup chopped fresh parsley	50 mL	

Cynthia Coop, Winnipeg designer, shared this recipe with me. Barley makes an interesting departure from rice in this mushroomy, herbed pilaf. It's best with a saucy dish; I recommend it for a buffet.

Melt 2 tbsp (25 mL) of butter in a large skillet. Add the nuts and cook over medium-low heat until golden. Remove with a slotted spoon and reserve.

Melt half the remaining butter in the pan; cook the onions and celery until translucent, 3 to 5 minutes. Remove with the slotted spoon and place in a 10-cup (2.5 L) casserole. Add the mushrooms to the pan and cook for 3 to 5 minutes or until they release their juices. Transfer to the casserole.

Melt the remaining butter in the pan; add the barley and fry, stirring frequently, for 5 minutes. All the grains should be coated with butter and they should be light gold in colour. Add to the casserole along with the stock, salt, pepper, bay leaf and thyme. Stir well; cover and bake at 350°F (180°C) for 45 to 60 minutes or until the barley is tender. (The slight squish the barley makes in your mouth adds another dimension to this casserole.)

Uncover, taste and adjust the seasoning if desired. Stir in the reserved almonds, dill and parsley.

Makes 10 servings.

Simmered Leeks and Tomatoes

⅓ cup oil	75 mL
2 cups sliced onions (3 medium)	500 mL
8 medium leeks (2 bunches)	8
2 cups chopped peeled tomatoes	500 mL
½ cup chicken stock	125 mL
1 tbsp chopped fresh dill or 1 tsp (5 mL) crumbled dried	15 mL
1 tsp chopped fresh mint or ½ tsp (2 mL) crumbled dried	5 mL
¼ tsp salt	1 mL
Pinch freshly ground pepper	Pinch
2 tbsp chopped fresh parsley or chervil	25 mL
⅓ cup freshly grated Parmesan cheese (optional)	75 mL

Serve this hot with sausages, any unsauced meat or grilled fish, or at room temperature as a light lunch dish.

In a heavy saucepan, heat oil and sauté onions for 5 to 8 minutes or until golden. Wash and trim the roots and leaves from leeks and cut each leek crosswise into 2-inch (5 cm) lengths. Add to pan along with the tomatoes, stock, dill, mint, salt and pepper. Mix gently to coat the leeks.

Bring to a boil. Cover, reduce heat and simmer gently until leeks are tender, 30 to 35 minutes, stirring occasionally. Taste and add more seasoning if desired.

Transfer vegetables to a shallow serving dish and sprinkle with parsley. If serving hot, sprinkle with grated cheese for a nice touch. Or serve at room temperature. You can even reheat.

Makes 6 servings.

Ann McColl Lindsay's Emotive Ratatouille

1 medium eggplant (12 oz/375 g)	1
3 small zucchini (12 oz/375 g total)	3
Salt	
1 large Spanish onion (8 oz/250 g)	1
2 large green bell peppers (12 oz/375 g total)	2
1 large sweet red bell pepper (6 oz/175 g)	1
6 large ripe tomatoes (2 lb/1 kg total)	6
1/4 cup olive oil	50 mL
3 large cloves garlic, minced	3
Freshly ground pepper	
2 tbsp chopped fresh marjoram or 1 1/2 tsp (7 mL) crumbled dried	25 mL
1 tbsp chopped fresh basil or 1 tsp (5 mL) crumbled dried	15 mL
Pinch cayenne	Pinch

In August and September, when baskets of tomatoes, eggplant, peppers and zucchini spill out in front of every greengrocer, take the time to make a batch of fragrant peasant vegetable stew. Ann McColl Lindsay's version is particularly flavourful. This is not unexpected — Ann, who owns one of the country's best cookware stores in London, Ontario, has few rivals in the expert use of herbs.

Wash vegetables. Trim and cut eggplant and zucchini into 1-inch (2.5 cm) cubes. Sprinkle with salt in a colander and let drain for 30 minutes.

Meanwhile, peel and slice onion thinly. Core, seed and chop peppers into 2-inch (5 cm) sections. Blanch tomatoes; peel and cut into wedges, removing and discarding seeds.

Rinse eggplant and zucchini and pat dry. In a large saucepan or sauteuse pan if, like Ann, you have one, heat half the oil with the garlic over medium-low heat. Add sliced onion, increase heat to medium and cook for 1 minute. Add vegetables in layers in the following order, cooking for 1 minute between additions: peppers, eggplant, zucchini and tomatoes.

Drizzle with remaining oil and season with salt, pepper, marjoram, basil and cayenne. Cover and simmer slowly on top of the stove for 1 hour or until vegetables are tender. Taste and adjust seasoning. You might like a sprinkle of fresh herbs at this time.

Serve as is, or spoon into a shallow gratin pan, then sprinkle generously with cheese (Gruyère, Romano, Parmesan or feta) and broil just long enough to melt and crisp the cheese.

Makes 8 lusty servings.

Spaghetti Squash with a Great Deal of Cheese

1 spaghetti squash (3 lb/1.35 kg)		1
3 tbsp butter		50 mL
⅓ cup finely chopped onion or shallots		75 mL
2 cups grated Gruyère cheese (6 oz/175 g)		500 mL
¾ tsp salt		4 mL
¼ tsp freshly ground pepper		1 mL
Pinch freshly grated nutmeg		Pinch
½ cup freshly grated Parmesan cheese		125 mL

With all the publicity spaghetti squash has received the last two or three years, it's unlikely anyone visiting a market stand would mistake this unusual-looking squash for any other vegetable. With cheese and butter, its long green strands are even better than fresh pasta.

Using an ice pick or skewer, prick to the centre of the squash in about 12 places. Set on a baking sheet and bake at 350°F (180°C) for 1½ hours, turning the squash over halfway through cooking time.

Cut off top third of squash lengthwise and spoon out the seeds and any liquid. Using a fork, scrape out the spaghetti-like strands from both bottom and top of the squash and set to drain in a sieve for 10 minutes. Discard top shell.

In a small skillet, melt butter and sauté onion until translucent, about 4 minutes. Transfer to a bowl and stir in the squash, Gruyère, salt, pepper and nutmeg. Taste and add more seasoning if necessary. Spoon into the bottom of the squash shell, sprinkle with Parmesan and set on the baking sheet. Bake at 350°F (180°C) for 25 to 30 minutes or until heated through and bubbly.

Makes 6 servings.

Baked Sweet Potato Squash with Tomatoes

3 lb sweet potato squash (or butternut)	1.35 kg
SAUCE:	
¼ cup oil or butter	50 mL
2 large cloves garlic, minced	2
1 cup finely chopped leeks or onions	250 mL
2 cups chopped, peeled tomatoes	500 mL
1 tsp salt	5 mL
¼ tsp freshly ground pepper	1 mL
TOPPING:	
¼ cup butter	50 mL
1½ cups fresh bread crumbs from Mediterranean-style bread	375 mL
2 tbsp finely chopped fresh parsley	25 mL

I chose this long pretty squash for two reasons: it's easy to peel, and its full flavour makes terrific eating, especially when combined with a second fall favourite, tomatoes.

Halve, peel and remove seeds from squash. Cut into slices about ¼ inch (5 mm) thick. Steam for 5 to 8 minutes or just until slices are tender but still hold their shape. Transfer to a shallow 6-cup (1.5 L) ovenproof dish (one suitable for gratins is best).

SAUCE: Heat oil for the sauce in a medium skillet and sauté garlic and leeks until translucent, about 4 minutes. Add tomatoes, salt and pepper. Cook, uncovered, over medium heat, stirring periodically until tomatoes have softened and blended with the other ingredients. Spread over squash.

TOPPING: Melt butter and combine with bread crumbs and parsley. Sprinkle evenly over vegetables.

Bake, uncovered, at 400°F (200°C) for 30 minutes or until squash is completely tender and topping is crisp and brown.

Makes 6 servings. You might like to add about 1 tsp (5 mL) of chopped fresh herbs to the tomato sauce; thyme, oregano, summer savory or marjoram is suitable.

SALADS

With a good dressing — a light fruity olive oil and wine vinegar or lemon juice — you can base a salad on almost any vegetable — fresh or dried beans, peppers, potatoes, tomatoes, even carrots and rutabaga. In areas of Canada settled by the Dutch or Germans, cream, sour cream or buttermilk replaces all or part of the oil, but the idea of one ingredient to coat the vegetables and another to provide a sour nip is still the basic equation. With this foundation, you can add highlights with mustard, garlic, fresh herbs, green onions or shallots.

For appetizers that can be prepared ahead of time, choose the hearty celery root and apple salad or the four pepper salad. Some salads pair nicely with main courses: the old-fashioned sour cream beans, for example, serves as a salad, while its dressing becomes a piquant sauce for barbecued pork tenderloin or ham. And you can count on salads using leafy fall greens or the hearts of curly endive for refreshing finales to dinners. Of course, some salads are all you really need for light meals. The chicken salad and the hearty white bean salad with lemon vinaigrette will fill the bill when served with thick slices of crusty bread.

Chicken Salad Deluxe

Whatever Rachel van Nostrand cooks tastes good. In her sunny kitchen in the Niagara Peninsula, she makes a truly fine chicken salad using a bird fresh from the barnyard. If you don't have your own chickens, buy a capon or roasting chicken and serve this salad for *alfresco* summer lunches or light suppers.

1 capon or roasting chicken (6 lb/2.7 kg)		1

CHICKEN STOCK:

2 cups	coarsely chopped onions (2 large)	500 mL
2 cups	chopped leeks, white and green parts (2 medium)	500 mL
$1\frac{1}{2}$ cups	chopped celery, leaves and tops (2 stalks)	375 mL

Cut the chicken into quarters; place in a deep stock pot and add cold water to cover the chicken $1\frac{1}{4}$ times. Add all the stock ingredients and bring to a boil. Reduce the heat to a simmer, carefully skimming off all the scum. Poach, un-

- 1½ cups chopped carrots (3 medium) 375 mL
- 2 bay leaves 2
- 4 tsp chopped fresh summer savory or 2 tsp (10 mL) crumbled dried 20 mL
- 1 tsp salt 5 mL
- ½ tsp coarsely crushed peppercorns 2 mL

SALAD:

- 2 hard-cooked eggs, chopped 2
- 1½ cups chopped celery heart 375 mL
- 1 cup diced celery root 250 mL
- ⅔ cup toasted slivered almonds 150 mL
- ½ cup lightly cooked fresh peas, snow peas or sugar pod peas 125 mL
- ½ cup finely chopped shallots 125 mL
- ¼ cup chopped black olives 50 mL
- ¼ cup chopped sweet pickle 50 mL
- 2 tsp chopped capers 10 mL
- 2 tsp each chopped fresh chervil and tarragon or 1 tsp (5 mL) crumbled dried 10 mL
- 1 cup mayonnaise, preferably homemade 250 mL
- 1 cup sour cream 250 mL
- Salt and freshly ground pepper

GARNISH:

- Shredded lettuce or watercress
- 1 melon or 3 or 4 peaches 1

covered, for 1½ to 2 hours or until tender.

Remove the chicken from the stock. Remove the skin and ease the meat from the bones, keeping it as intact and in as large pieces as possible. Place the meat in a deep bowl; cover with 1 cup (250 mL) of the stock and refrigerate.

Return the skin and bones to the stock pot and boil vigorously for 20 to 30 minutes or until the liquid is reduced to about 8 cups (2 L). Strain and use this naturally jellied stock for aspics or freeze in small portions for soup.

To make the salad, remove the chicken from the stock; drain and chop coarsely. Combine with all the salad ingredients. Taste and add more herbs if desired. Cover and keep chilled.

To serve, scoop the salad onto a bed of shredded lettuce and garnish with slices of melon or peach. When nasturtiums are in bloom, chop a few leaves into the salad and nestle a bloom or two by the fruit.

Makes 8 to 10 servings.

White Kidney Bean Salad with Lemon Vinaigrette

SALAD:

1 cup dry white kidney beans (8 oz/250 g)	250 mL
⅔ cup chopped green onions	150 mL
⅓ cup chopped red pepper or pimiento	75 mL
¼ cup chopped fresh parsley	50 mL
2 cans (each 6.5 oz/184 g) solid white tuna, drained	2

DRESSING:

½ cup olive oil	125 mL
¼ cup fresh lemon juice	50 mL
2 large cloves garlic, minced	2
1 tsp salt	5 mL
½ tsp coarsely ground pepper	2 mL

GARNISH:

1 lemon	1
½ cup red pepper strips or pimiento	125 mL

Beans make a delicious cold salad when emboldened with a garlicky oil and lemon juice dressing, and garnished with pimiento for colour and taste. Serve as part of an antipasto platter or with cold roast beef or any grilled or roasted lamb. For a quicker salad, substitute drained canned white kidney beans, using two 19 oz (540 mL) cans.

Place beans in a small saucepan with enough cold water to cover by 3 inches (7 cm). Bring to a boil, uncovered, and boil moderately hard for 2 minutes. Remove from heat, cover and let stand for 1 hour. Drain, rinse and cover with same quantity of fresh cold water. Add a pinch of salt. Bring to a boil, cover and simmer until tender, 20 to 30 minutes. Drain well, let cool and transfer to a large bowl. Add onions, red pepper and parsley. Separate tuna into large chunks and add to bowl.

DRESSING: Combine all the ingredients for the dressing. Pour over salad and toss. Cover and chill if making in advance but bring to room temperature before serving. Taste and adjust seasoning.

Transfer salad to an attractive bowl. Slice lemon thinly and remove seeds. Halve and use to garnish the outside edge of the salad. Arrange red pepper in a star in the middle.

Makes 6 servings.

Bistro-Style Warm Potato Salad

9 medium-large potatoes (3 lb/1.35 kg total), red-skinned ones if possible	9
¼ cup chicken stock	50 mL

A wintertime bistro lunch at l'Express on Rue St-Denis in Montreal consists of a mound of this zesty warm salad, along with hot sliced garlic sausage, a bouquet of fresh watercress and a dollop of coarse grained Pommery mustard.

$\frac{1}{4}$ cup white wine vinegar	50 mL
1 tbsp dry white wine	15 mL
1 tsp salt	5 mL
$\frac{1}{4}$ tsp coarsely ground pepper	1 mL
$\frac{1}{3}$ cup olive oil	75 mL
$1\frac{1}{2}$ tsp coarse grained Pommery mustard	7 mL
$\frac{1}{4}$ cup finely chopped fresh parsley	50 mL
$\frac{3}{4}$ cup thinly sliced Spanish onion rings	175 mL

Scrub potatoes and cook, covered, in a saucepan of boiling salted water until tender but still firm. Drain; dry briefly over low heat and peel if desired. Cut neatly into $\frac{1}{2}$-inch (1 cm) slices and place in a large shallow bowl. While still warm, sprinkle with stock, vinegar, wine, salt and pepper. Turn gently.

Combine oil, mustard and parsley; drizzle evenly over potatoes, turning gently to coat the slices on both sides. Taste and adjust seasoning. Arrange attractively in a serving dish, garnish with onion rings and serve.

Makes 6 generous servings.

Celery Root with Apples and Toasted Almonds

Look for celery root (or "celeriac") among the root vegetables. It's the hairy, rutabaga-sized vegetable with a mild, nutty, celery flavour and firm texture. It's a natural with apples and almonds, and makes a light appetizer or fine side dish with grilled fish or pork chops.

1 celery root (1 lb/500 g)	1
2 tbsp lemon juice	25 mL
3 large crisp apples	3
$\frac{1}{4}$ cup coarsely chopped Spanish onion	50 mL
$\frac{2}{3}$ cup mayonnaise	150 mL
2 tbsp sour cream	25 mL
1 tsp Dijon mustard	5 mL
Salt and freshly ground pepper	
$\frac{3}{4}$ cup unblanched almonds	175 mL

Trim and peel celery root. Chop neatly into matchstick pieces by hand or use a very coarse shredder or food processor with julienne attachment. There should be about 3 cups (750 mL). Immediately toss with lemon juice to prevent darkening. Quarter, core and dice apples; mix apples and onion with the celery root and lemon juice.

Blend together mayonnaise, sour cream and mustard. Stir into salad to coat all pieces evenly. Taste and season with salt and pepper.

Spread almonds in a single layer in a pan. Toast at 350°F (180°C) until lightly browned, about 10 minutes, watching carefully and stirring to prevent burning. Chop into slivers.

To serve, arrange salad in a bowl and garnish with almonds.

Makes 6 servings.

Fall Greens with Garlic Yogurt Dressing

SALAD:

1 heart curly chicory	1
1 heart escarole	1
1 head radicchio	1
1 head Belgian endive	1
1 bunch watercress	1
⅔ cup grated Gruyère cheese	150 mL

DRESSING:

1 clove garlic	1
¾ tsp salt	4 mL
¼ tsp freshly ground pepper	1 mL
½ tsp coarse grained Pommery mustard	2 mL
4 tsp white wine vinegar	20 mL
1 tbsp olive oil	15 mL
½ cup natural yogurt	125 mL
¼ cup buttermilk	50 mL

In the late summer and fall, light green curly chicory and escarole make delightful salads. A few leaves of radicchio, a curly, purplish red endive, not only look handsome but add a nice bite. Make the yogurt dressing at least 4 hours before serving so the flavours will blend.

Separate the leaves and rinse the chicory, escarole and radicchio. Break the chicory and escarole leaves in two. Simply wipe the outside leaves of Belgian endive with a damp cloth and separate. Remove the coarse stems from the watercress. Wrap greens separately in paper towels and chill.

DRESSING: Crush the garlic with the salt. Whisk together in a small bowl with the pepper, mustard, vinegar, oil, yogurt and buttermilk. Chill for 4 hours to mature the flavours. Taste and adjust seasoning if desired.

Line a large salad bowl with the curly chicory and escarole. Set the radicchio and endive inside the escarole and fill the middle with the watercress. Sprinkle the cheese over the chicory and escarole.

Drizzle the dressing over the salad and bring to the table for everyone to admire. Toss.

Makes 10 generous servings.

Sour Cream Bean Salad

1 lb green beans	500 g
⅓ cup finely chopped onion	75 mL
¾ tsp salt	4 mL
1 tbsp granulated sugar	15 mL
¼ tsp freshly ground pepper	1 mL

My aunt Margaret Davis used to serve bowls of sour cream bean salad along side a Sunday dinner roast pork. The sour cream is a delicious reminder of the influence of the many German settlers in Perth County, Ontario.

Wash, trim and cook beans in boiling salted water until tender-crisp, 6 to 8 minutes. Drain and refresh under cold

3/4 cup sour cream	175 mL
1 tbsp cider vinegar	15 mL

running water and cut into 2-inch (5 cm) lengths. Set on towels.

Place onion in a bowl and sprinkle with 1/4 tsp (1 mL) of the salt. Let stand for 10 minutes. Drain and pat with paper towels to absorb moisture.

In a large bowl, combine the remaining salt, sugar, pepper, sour cream and vinegar. Add onion and beans; toss well, cover and chill until serving time.

This salad can be made a day in advance and is terrific for a picnic (remember to keep it chilled). It's good with sausages, smoked pork chops, cold poached fish, roast chicken, steaks and burgers.

Makes 6 servings.

Garlic Artichokes

Joe Carlino introduced me to these garlicky artichokes that his family serves as part of their Easter feast. One large juicy clove of garlic per artichoke is sufficient, though two cloves would be appreciated by garlic lovers. The artichoke and garlic flavours blend into an elusive sweetness.

6 artichokes (6 oz/175 g each)	6
6 large cloves garlic	6
2 cups fine dry bread crumbs	500 mL
1 tsp salt	5 mL
1/4 cup olive oil	50 mL
Water	

Rinse artichokes in cold water and trim each stem even with the base. Holding the base in your hand, bang the pointed tip firmly onto the counter 3 or 4 times (this helps separate the leaves). Being very careful of the thistle-sharp tips, separate the leaves so the artichoke looks like a half-open flower. Repeat with remaining artichokes.

Peel and sliver the garlic. Dividing them equally among the artichokes, push garlic slivers and bread crumbs to the base of the leaves and sprinkle with salt.

Place the artichokes base down in a single layer in a large saucepan. Drizzle with the oil and pour enough water into the pan to come 1 inch (2.5 cm) up the sides of the 'chokes.

Cover and bring to a boil. Reduce heat and simmer for 1 hour or until a leaf can be pulled out without resistance. Uncover and let cool in the pan. Remove with tongs, drain briefly and serve on salad plates. Set a large plate on the table to receive the remains of the leaves.

Makes 6 servings. Can also be served as an appetizer.

Marinated Garden Salad

Here is a veritable garden in a bowl. It's excellent fare for a picnic or a summer buffet. You can vary the mix of vegetables according to your harvest.

DRESSING:

1/3 cup white wine vinegar	75 mL
1 cup olive oil	250 mL
1 tsp salt	5 mL
1/4 tsp freshly ground pepper	1 mL
1 tsp Dijon mustard	5 mL
1/4 cup finely chopped fresh chives or green onions	50 mL
2 tbsp finely chopped fresh parsley	25 mL
1 tsp each chopped fresh basil, marjoram and thyme or 1/2 tsp (2 mL) crumbled dried	5 mL
1 clove garlic, minced	1

VEGETABLES:

10 small carrots (8 oz/250 g total)	10
3 small white turnips (12 oz/375 g total)	3
1 small rutabaga (1 lb/500 g)	1
4 cups cauliflower florets (1 small head)	1 L
4 cups broccoli florets (8 oz/250 g)	1 L
4 cups green beans, cut into 2-inch (5 cm) lengths (12 oz/375 g)	1 L
2 cups snow peas or sugar pod peas (4 oz/125 g)	500 mL
8 cups boiling water	2 L
1 tsp salt	5 mL

DRESSING: Combine all the ingredients and set aside.

VEGETABLES: Scrub the carrots, scrape if necessary and quarter lengthwise. Cut in half crosswise to make sticks about 3 inches (7 cm) long. Peel the turnips and rutabaga and cut into even sticks 3 x 1/2 inches (7 x 1 cm). Prepare the cauliflower, broccoli and green beans. Trim the stem end off the snow peas and pull out the string from the straight side. Keep the vegetables in separate piles.

Pour the boiling water and salt into a medium saucepan. Boil each vegetable separately, one after the other in the salted water in the following order, covering the saucepan during the cooking: the carrots for 3 minutes, the turnips and rutabagas for 5 minutes, the cauliflower for 3 to 4 minutes, the broccoli for 3 to 4 minutes, the green beans for 4 minutes and, finally, the snow peas for 30 seconds (sugar pod peas take 2 to 3 minutes). Test the vegetables as they cook and remove them if they are ready before the suggested time.

As soon as each vegetable is tender-crisp, remove them from the boiling water with a slotted spoon and immediately plunge into cold water. This stops the vegetables from cooking further and helps set their colours. When each vegetable is chilled, immediately scoop out of the water and drain thoroughly on paper towels. Pat dry.

Transfer the vegetables to a large bowl. Pour on the dressing and toss very gently. Cover and chill for 2 to 12 hours, tossing once or twice to marinate all the vegetables evenly.

Makes 12 to 15 servings.

Marinated Four Pepper Salad

SALAD:

1 large head romaine lettuce	1
4 large sweet red bell or shepherd peppers	4
2 large green peppers, preferably Cubanelle	2
2 large yellow peppers	2
6 large banana peppers, preferably hot	6

DRESSING:

½ cup olive oil	125 mL
3 tbsp red wine vinegar	50 mL
1 tsp salt	5 mL
¼ tsp freshly ground pepper	1 mL
¼ tsp paprika	1 mL
¼ tsp coriander	1 mL
1 large glove garlic, minced	1
2 tbsp finely chopped onion	25 mL

The array of peppers available from August to November is an invitation to enjoy them in salads in both their raw and roasted states. They're almost irresistible roasted and make a good appetizer as well as a salad.

There are several easy ways to roast peppers. You can broil them 4 inches (10 cm) from the heat, or set them on a rack over an electric element, turning the peppers as they blister and char. If you need only a few peppers for garnish, spear with a long-handled fork and char in a surface gas flame. Whatever method you use to roast the peppers, they'll be easier to peel if you set them aside in a covered container for 10 minutes after roasting. A saucepan, a casserole dish, even a paper bag will do.

Discard rough outer leaves from lettuce. Separate and wash leaves. Spin or pat dry. Wrap in paper towel, place in a plastic bag and refrigerate.

Roast peppers, one kind at a time, according to the instructions above (note the thin-skinned Cubanelle and banana peppers char more quickly than the bell variety). Steam for 10 minutes in a closed saucepan. Cut out stem ends; peel, slit and discard membranes and seeds. Rinse off any sticky seeds and patches of charred skin. Pat dry.

Cut roasted peppers into strips about ½ inch (1 cm) wide, keeping each kind of pepper in a separate bowl.

DRESSING: Combine all ingredients for the dressing. Shake well and pour a third over each bowl of peppers. Cover and marinate peppers in the dressing for 1 to 2 hours at room temperature, stirring periodically.

Line a bowl, preferably rectangular, with about 12 of the finest romaine leaves. Arrange the peppers in 4 bands in the bowl and serve. Encourage guests to mix varieties as they help themselves.

Makes 10 to 12 servings.

Red Pepper and Broccoli Salad

This is a highly flavoured salad that exploits the vivid reds and greens of these fall vegetables.

DRESSING:

¼ cup red wine vinegar	50 mL
⅔ cup olive oil	150 mL
2 tsp Dijon mustard	10 mL
1 clove garlic, crushed	1
2 tbsp finely chopped fresh parsley	25 mL
1 tsp finely chopped fresh oregano or ½ tsp (2 mL) crumbled dried	5 mL
1 tsp salt	5 mL
¼ tsp freshly ground pepper	1 mL

SALAD:

4 oz button mushrooms	125 g
1 bunch broccoli (1 lb/500 g)	1
2 large sweet red peppers (12 oz/375 g total)	2
3 oz feta cheese	100 g
12 black olives	12
3 thin slices red onion	3

DRESSING: Combine all ingredients for the dressing in a medium bowl. Wipe the mushrooms with a damp cloth and add to the dressing. Let stand at room temperature for 1 to 2 hours.

SALAD: Cut the broccoli into florets. Peel the stalks and cut into finger-sized strips. Blanch the florets for 1 minute, the strips for 1½ minutes, in a large pan of rapidly boiling water. Immediately immerse broccoli in cold water to halt cooking. Drain thoroughly on paper towels, wrap and chill. Remove the stems, seeds and membranes from the peppers and cut into strips. Wrap and chill.

To serve, arrange the broccoli in a salad bowl. Crumble the cheese and mound in the middle. Surround the cheese with the olives. Using a slotted spoon, remove the mushrooms from the dressing and place around the olives. Separate the onion rings and alternate them with the pepper strips over the rest of the broccoli. Drizzle with the dressing. Bring the salad to the table, toss and serve.

Makes 6 generous servings.

Heart of Curly Endive with Walnuts and Blue Cheese

The mild tender hearts of curly endive or escarole blend particularly well with crunchy walnuts and nippy blue cheese. Serve in the fall and winter with a hearty soup or an egg dish such as an omelet, quiche or frittata.

SALAD:

2 heads curly endive (12 oz/375 g each)	2
½ cup chopped, freshly shelled walnuts	125 mL
½ cup crumbled blue cheese (2 oz/60 g)	125 mL

Remove coarse outer leaves from curly endive and break

DRESSING:

⅓ cup olive oil	75 mL
1 tbsp walnut oil (optional but nice)	15 mL
2 tbsp white wine or cider vinegar	25 mL
½ tsp salt	2 mL
Pinch freshly ground pepper	Pinch
1 tsp Dijon mustard	5 mL

the frilly white or light yellow leaves and green heart into bite-sized pieces. Arrange attractively in a shallow salad bowl. Sprinkle with walnuts and cheese.

DRESSING: Combine all the ingredients for the dressing. Shake well and drizzle over the salad. Bring to the table and toss; taste for seasoning and serve.

Makes 6 to 8 servings.

Summer Tomato Salad

Tomatoes and cheese taste great together, especially in a salad drizzled with a zesty vinaigrette. Any sharp cheese is good; I recommend old white Cheddar, feta, smoked mozzarella, crumbly blue cheese or chèvre.

SALAD:

6 romaine lettuce leaves	6
4 medium-large tomatoes (1¼lb/625 g total)	4
1 tbsp each finely chopped fresh parsley and basil	15 mL
⅓ cup grated or crumbled cheese (see above)	75 mL

VINAIGRETTE:

3 tbsp olive oil	50 mL
2 tsp wine vinegar	10 mL
½ tsp salt	2 mL
¼ tsp freshly ground black pepper	1 mL
¼ tsp Dijon mustard	1 mL
1 clove garlic, minced	1

Line a serving platter with lettuce leaves. Core the tomatoes and slice vertically. Arrange the tomatoes on the lettuce, then sprinkle with parsley, basil and grated cheese.

VINAIGRETTE: Combine all the ingredients for the dressing. Drizzle over the salad and serve immediately.

Makes 6 servings.

DESSERTS

In previous centuries, Canadians burned up enough energy scrubbing, logging, ploughing and paddling to justify the consumption of thousands of calories in pies, cookies, cakes and puddings. In fact, a sweet course on the table every day was a sign that a family had made it in the new land.

Our lifestyles have changed, but the Canadian sweet tooth persists. Where once we earned our daily bread with manual labour, now we puff through a jog or swim to earn our daily torte or ice cream.

But some things never change. Servings at dessert may be smaller today, but I think most Canadians can still discern that made-from-scratch desserts are worth the effort they take. Baking is a timeless art, one Canadian cooks of all backgrounds cherish. The baker whose blueberry pie crust is flaky and tender, whose lemon cardamom pound cake is high and even, whose old-fashioned fruit and nut bars are moist and chewy, is a true craftsperson in the kitchen.

Whenever anyone tells me there's no such thing as Canadian cooking, I tell them the tradition that lives on in pastry, cake and cookie-making alone gives Canada a national cuisine, one made all the richer by regional specialties such as *tarte au sucre* from Quebec or apple platz from Manitoba. Our sweet-making skills are a national treasure that should not be lightly dismissed, or debased with packaged shortcuts. These skills were handed down to us by our mothers, and should be passed on to our children in turn.

Apple Platz

DOUGH:

2 cups all-purpose flour	500 mL
1 tsp soda	5 mL
¼ tsp salt	1 mL
½ cup butter	125 mL
1 egg	1
½ cup (approx) milk	125 mL

FILLING:

4 cups chopped, peeled, cored apples	1 L
1 tsp grated lemon peel	5 mL
2 tsp lemon juice	10 mL
1½ cups granulated sugar	375 mL
½ cup all-purpose flour	125 mL
Pinch salt	Pinch
2 eggs	2
½ cup butter, melted	125 mL

A few years ago, I enjoyed a square of rhubarb platz in Steinbach, Manitoba, the heart of that province's Russian Mennonite community. Platz is served with morning coffee, as a luncheon dessert and as a *faspa* (afternoon snack). It's somewhere between a pie and a cake with a crumb topping. Because of their availability, rhubarb and apple fill most platz, but cooks can use any plentiful seasonal fruit, such as gooseberries, cherries, apricots, strawberries or a combination.

Grease a 9-inch square (2.5 L) cake pan and set aside.

In a large bowl, combine flour, soda and salt. With a pastry blender or 2 knives, cut in butter until mixture is crumbly. In a separate bowl, beat egg; drizzle over dry ingredients and toss together with a fork to make coarse crumbs. Scoop out 1 cup (250 mL) and reserve.

Sprinkle milk over remaining crumbs; stir together to make a soft dough. Use a little more milk if necessary to achieve this consistency. Spread into prepared pan.

FILLING: Combine apples, lemon peel and juice in a large bowl. Add sugar, flour and salt and toss together. In a separate bowl, beat eggs and mix in butter. Stir into apple mixture. Pour over platz base in pan. Sprinkle reserved crumbs over fruit filling.

Bake at 350°F (180°C) for 50 to 60 minutes or until the platz has risen evenly, the crumbs have taken on a golden tinge and a skewer inserted in the filling in the centre of the pan comes out clean. Let cool in the pan; best served within a day or two.

Makes 12 pieces.

Rolled Oats Cake with Broiled Coconut Topping

1 cup regular rolled oats	250 mL
1½ cups boiling water	375 mL
½ cup butter	125 mL
1¾ cups firmly packed brown sugar	425 mL
2 eggs	2
1 tsp vanilla	5 mL
1½ cups all-purpose flour	375 mL
1 tsp soda	5 mL
½ tsp salt	2 mL
½ tsp freshly grated nutmeg	2 mL
½ tsp cinnamon	2 mL

TOPPING:

¼ cup butter	50 mL
½ cup firmly packed brown sugar	125 mL
3 tbsp light cream	50 mL
¾ cup shredded coconut, preferably unsweetened	175 mL

From Prince Edward Island comes this spicy moist cake, also known as Queen Elizabeth Cake; it's perfect for lunches and snacks.

Grease a 9-inch square (2.5 L) cake pan and set aside.

In a small bowl, combine rolled oats and water; let stand for 20 minutes. In a large bowl, cream together butter and brown sugar until light and fluffy. Beat in eggs, 1 at a time. Add vanilla and oats mixture. Sift together flour, soda, salt, nutmeg and cinnamon; mix into batter.

Transfer batter to prepared pan, using a scraper to make the batter higher at the edges of the pan. Bake at 350°F (180°C) for 55 minutes or until the cake springs back when lightly touched in the centre.

Meanwhile, prepare the topping. Cream together butter and brown sugar. Mix in cream and coconut. Remove cake from oven; turn on broiler. Spread coconut mixture evenly and gently over hot cake. Arrange oven rack so top of cake is about 4 inches (10 cm) from heat. Broil for 2 to 3 minutes or until topping is slightly browned and bubbly. Remove from oven and let cool; store in pan until needed.

Makes 20 pieces.

Note: This cake will stay moist, if well wrapped, for up to 1 week. It also freezes well and is always appreciated in lunches or as an after-school snack.

Lunar Rhubarb Cake

½ cup butter	125 mL
1½ cups granulated sugar	375 mL
1 egg	1
1 tsp vanilla	5 mL
2 cups all-purpose flour	500 mL
1 tsp soda	5 mL
½ tsp salt	2 mL
2 cups chopped rhubarb, in ½-inch (1 cm) pieces	500 mL
1 cup buttermilk	250 mL

TOPPING:

¼ cup butter	50 mL
2 tsp cinnamon	10 mL
1 cup firmly packed brown sugar	250 mL

Sandy Hall, a cooking school supervisor from Mississauga, Ontario, shared this recipe with me for *Canadian Living* magazine. We named it lunar cake because its surface looks like a moonscape, with the buttery brown sugar topping dipping down into the cake and crusting over the surface.

This cake is big enough for a crowd or a bake sale. Or you can enjoy half of it now and freeze the rest for later.

Grease a 13 x 9-inch (4 L) cake pan and set aside.

Beat together butter and granulated sugar until smooth and creamy. Blend in egg and vanilla.

Stir together flour, soda, and salt. Scoop out 2 tbsp (25 mL) and use to dredge rhubarb. Mix dry ingredients into the creamed batter in 3 parts, alternating with the buttermilk in 2 parts. Gently stir in rhubarb. Spoon into prepared pan and smooth the surface.

TOPPING: Blend together all the topping ingredients and sprinkle evenly over the batter.

Bake at 350°F (180°C) for 45 minutes or until the cake has risen and browned, has come away from the sides of the pan and a skewer inserted in the middle comes out clean.

Makes 18 servings.

Apple Custard Cake Deluxe

½ cup unsalted butter, melted	125 mL
1 cup granulated sugar	250 mL
2 eggs	2
1 tsp grated orange or lemon peel	5 mL
1¾ cups all-purpose flour	425 mL
2 tsp baking powder	10 mL
¼ tsp salt	1 mL
6 large apples (2 lb/1 kg)	6
2 tsp cinnamon	10 mL

TOPPING:

½ cup unsalted butter	125 mL
1 cup granulated sugar	250 mL
2 eggs	2

Based on an apple torte from the *Naomi Cook Book* published in 1948, this is the best version I know of high apple cake.

Northern Spy and Wealthy apples are recommended.

Grease a 9-inch (3 L) springform pan and set aside.

To make the batter, pour melted butter into a large bowl. Gradually beat in sugar, then eggs, one at a time, and orange peel.

Stir together flour, baking powder and salt. Mix gently into batter. Spread into prepared pan.

Peel, core and cut apples into eighths. There should be 8 cups (2 L). Set 2 apple pieces on their sides in the batter in the centre of the cake. Stick remaining apple pieces upright in the batter around the centre leaning the pieces toward the centre. The top of the cake should look like a chrysanthemum. Sprinkle with cinnamon and bake at 350°F (180°C) for 1 hour. Then add topping.

TOPPING: Cream together butter and sugar. Beat in eggs and pour over apples. Return to oven for 20 minutes or until topping is firm and apples are cooked through (test with skewer).

Set cake pan on a rack and let cool. Remove sides of pan. This cake is beautifully moist and should be removed from the pan if stored overnight to prevent discolouration of pan.

Serves 12 to 16.

Black Currant and Orange Sour Cream Coffee Cake

1 cup unsalted butter	250 mL
2 cups granulated sugar	500 mL
4 eggs	4
2¾ cups all-purpose flour	675 mL
1½ tsp baking powder	7 mL
1 tsp cinnamon	5 mL
½ tsp soda	2 mL
½ tsp salt	2 mL
¼ tsp ground cloves	1 mL
2 cups fresh black currants	500 mL
1 cup slivered blanched almonds	250 mL
1 tbsp coarsely grated orange peel	15 mL
1 cup sour cream	250 mL

GLAZE:

¼ cup orange juice	50 mL
¼ cup granulated sugar	50 mL
1 tbsp orange liqueur (optional)	15 mL

Black currants give a fresh summery taste to an old classic.

Grease a 9-inch (3 L) tube pan and set aside.

Cream together butter and sugar until light and fluffy. Add eggs, one at a time, beating well after each addition.

Blend together flour, baking powder, cinnamon, soda, salt and cloves. Stir in currants, almonds and orange peel. Stir into batter in 3 parts, alternating with sour cream in 2 parts.

Scrape batter into prepared pan, tapping pan lightly on the counter to release air bubbles. Bake at 325°F (160°C) for 1½ hours or until the cake has come away from the sides of the pan and a skewer inserted in the middle of the cake comes out clean. Let cool in the pan for 10 minutes, then turn out onto a rack and set right side up.

GLAZE: In a small saucepan, heat together juice and sugar until syrupy. Stir in liqueur if using. While the cake is still warm, use a skewer to make about 25 holes about 2 inches (5 cm) deep in top of cake. Drizzle orange syrup over top of cake and let cool completely. Serve immediately or freeze.

Makes 1 large cake that can be cut into 20 pieces.

The Campbell Lemon Cream Sponge Cake

When Mabel Campbell was growing up in the Ottawa Valley town of Kemptville in the '20s and '30s, fine cakes were part of every social occasion. Mrs. Campbell still makes a true lemon sponge cake that harks back to that era, and she has passed on her skill to daughter Mary. This is Mary Campbell's adaptation of her mother's recipe. Both Campbells serve this cake with fresh strawberries in season.

CAKE:

6 eggs	6
1 cup granulated sugar	250 mL
1 tsp grated lemon peel	5 mL
1 tbsp lemon juice	15 mL
1 cup cake and pastry flour	250 mL
¼ tsp salt	1 mL

LEMON FILLING:

3 tbsp cornstarch	50 mL
1 cup granulated sugar	250 mL
Pinch salt	Pinch
2 cups water	500 mL
2 tsp grated lemon peel	10 mL
2 egg yolks	2
⅓ cup lemon juice	75 mL
1 tbsp butter	15 mL
1 egg white	1

VANILLA WHIPPED CREAM:

1 cup whipping cream	250 mL
2 tsp granulated sugar	10 mL
1 tsp vanilla	5 mL

CAKE: Grease and flour the bottom but not the sides of a 9-inch (3 L) tube pan and set aside.

Separate eggs, dropping the whites into a large bowl and yolks into a medium one. Beat whites to soft peaks and continue to beat at high speed, gradually adding half the sugar. Beat until whites have tripled in volume and stand in firm glossy peaks.

Beat yolks, gradually adding the rest of the sugar, lemon peel and juice. Beat until the yolks have doubled in volume, are light yellow in colour and fall from the beaters in ribbons.

Gently fold yolk mixture into whites. Combine flour and salt and sift about ¼ of it over the batter. Fold in gently and repeat 3 more times until all flour is incorporated. Transfer to prepared pan. To eliminate air bubbles, run the blade of a dinner knife through the batter 3 times, once around each edge and once through the middle.

Bake at 350°F (180°C) for 45 to 55 minutes or until cake begins to come away from the pan, springs back when lightly touched and when a skewer inserted into the cake comes out clean. Invert cake pan with centre tube over a large bottle or stand on elevated legs or centre post (on chiffon cake pans). Let cool completely.

To finish cake, turn right side up. Loosen cake and turn out onto a cake plate. Brush off loose crumbs and use a serrated knife to slice cake horizontally into 3 equal layers.

FILLING: Combine cornstarch and all but 1 tbsp (15 mL) sugar in a heavy saucepan. Add salt, water and lemon peel, stirring to blend smoothly. Cook over medium heat, stirring constantly, until mixture thickens and clears. Reduce heat and simmer, stirring frequently, for 8 minutes.

Beat yolks. Add about ½ cup (125 mL) cornstarch mixture to yolks, then transfer warmed yolks to remaining cornstarch mixture and cook over very low heat for 2 to 3 minutes or until thick and smooth. Add lemon juice and butter; remove from heat and let cool completely.

Beat egg white until soft peaks form. Add remaining sugar and beat to firm glossy peaks. Fold into lemon filling.

Reassemble cake, spreading about ⅔ of the lemon filling between layers. Spread a thin layer of the remaining filling over top and sides of cake and spoon any extra into the centre. Refrigerate.

WHIPPED CREAM: Whip cream; blend in sugar and vanilla. Spread over top and sides of iced cake just before serving. For a slightly firmer set or if icing cake ahead of time, sprinkle 1 tsp (5 mL) unflavoured gelatin over whipping cream before beating.

Makes about 12 servings.

Pumpkin Cream Roll

3 eggs	3
1 cup granulated sugar	250 mL
⅔ cup puréed pumpkin	150 mL
1 tsp lemon juice	5 mL
1 cup cake and pastry flour	250 mL
1 tsp baking powder	5 mL
¼ tsp salt	1 mL
2 tsp cinnamon	10 mL
1 tsp ginger	5 mL
½ tsp freshly grated nutmeg	2 mL
¼ cup icing sugar	50 mL

CREAM FILLING:

¾ cup cream cheese (6 oz/175 g)	175 mL
¼ cup unsalted butter	50 mL
1 cup icing sugar, sifted	250 mL
Pinch salt	Pinch
½ tsp vanilla	2 mL
¾ cup chopped pecans	175 mL
2 tbsp icing sugar for garnish	25 mL

This is pumpkin without the pie. It's a rolled, spiced pumpkin sponge cake with a pecan and cream cheese filling — a perfect make-ahead dessert for a Thanksgiving weekend.

Grease a 15 x 10-inch (2 L) jelly roll pan. Line bottom with waxed paper; grease paper and set aside.

In a large bowl, beat eggs at high speed until thick and light in colour, about 5 minutes. Continue to beat, gradually adding the granulated sugar. Blend in pumpkin purée and lemon juice.

Sift together flour, baking powder, salt and spices over the batter and blend together.

Spread batter evenly in prepared pan. Bake at 350°F (180°C) for 15 to 18 minutes or until cake springs back when lightly touched and has shrunk away a little from the sides of the pan.

Sprinkle icing sugar over the surface of the cake. Cover with a clean tea towel and immediately flip the cake out onto the towel. Remove the waxed paper and roll the cake lengthwise in the towel. Place on a rack until completely cool.

CREAM FILLING: Beat together cream cheese and butter until soft. Mix in 1 cup (250 mL) icing sugar, salt and vanilla. Beat until fluffy and smooth. Unroll the cake, spread evenly with filling and sprinkle with pecans. Roll up the cake again and set on a long serving plate. Cover and keep chilled until serving time.

To serve, sift the 2 tbsp (25 mL) icing sugar over the top of the cake and cut into slices about 1¼ inches (3 cm) thick.

Makes about 10 servings.

Lemon Cardamom Pound Cake

rants	250 mL
arsely grated peel	15 mL
arsely grated peel	15 mL
alted butter	250 mL
ıulated sugar	250 mL
la	5 mL
	6
ɔurpose flour	500 mL
lamom	15 mL
g powder	10 mL
	Pinch

NG (OPTIONAL):

ulated sugar	50 mL
1 tbsp coarsely grated lemon peel	15 mL
¼ cup lemon juice	50 mL

Lemon and cardamom give this elegant pound cake its elusive flavour. Use a zester to get coarsely grated citrus peel. The syrup topping adds more lemon flavour to the cake and keeps it moist. However, the cake is irresistible even without the syrup.

Grease a 9 x 5-inch (2 L) loaf pan and dust lightly with flour or line with waxed paper and grease lightly. Set aside.

Place currants in a sieve over a saucepan of simmering water and steam until softened, 5 to 10 minutes. Remove currants, pat dry and combine with the orange and lemon peel.

In a large bowl, cream together butter, sugar and vanilla. Beat in eggs, one at a time. The batter may curdle but this does not affect the loaf.

Stir together flour, cardamom, baking powder and salt. Scoop out about 2 tbsp (25 mL) and dredge the currants and peel. Stir the rest of the flour mixture into the batter, mixing just until smooth. Stir in currants and rind and transfer to prepared pan.

Bake at 350°F (180°C) for 1 hour or until a skewer inserted into the middle comes out clean.

SYRUP TOPPING: As soon as the cake comes out of the oven, use a wide skewer to make about 20 holes about 2 inches (5 cm) deep in the top of the cake. Combine syrup ingredients and drizzle over cake. Let cool in pan. With or without syrup, store the cake for 1 day before slicing. It also freezes well.

Makes about 12 slices.

Sour Cream Pecan Torte

1 cup unsalted butter	250 mL
1 cup granulated sugar	250 mL
1½ tsp grated lemon peel	7 mL
2 eggs	2
1¾ cups all-purpose flour	425 mL
2 tsp baking powder	10 mL
¼ tsp salt	1 mL

FILLING:

2½ cups sour cream	625 mL
1 tsp each vanilla and brandy	5 mL
¾ cup icing sugar	175 mL
2¼ cups very finely chopped pecans	550 mL

This is a cake that's easy to make and deserves to be widely known. Buttery, thin, cookie-like layers are sandwiched together with a sour cream and nut filling that moistens and mellows the layers. Let the cake stand for one day before cutting.

Grease four 9-inch (1.5 L) round cake pans. Line the bottoms with waxed paper circles cut to fit; grease the waxed paper and set pans aside. (If you have only 2 pans of this size, prepare 4 waxed paper circles and bake the cakes 2 at a time.)

Cream the butter until fluffy; gradually beat in the sugar, lemon peel and eggs, one at a time.

Mix together flour, baking powder and salt and stir into the batter in 3 parts. Divide the batter equally between the 4 pans and spread thinly. Bake at 350°F (180°C) for 8 to 10 minutes or until the layers spring back when lightly touched and are golden brown on the bottom. Let cool for 5 minutes. Remove from pans and let cool completely on racks. Peel off the paper.

FILLING: Combine the sour cream, vanilla, brandy, icing sugar and 2 cups (500 mL) of the pecans. Set 1 of the cake layers on a serving plate. Spread ¼ of the filling over the layer, leaving a ¼-inch (5 mm) border uncovered around the edge. Cover with the second layer and continue with the filling and layers, finishing with filling. Spread top layer of filling right to the edge of the cake and sprinkle remaining nuts around the edge. Cover and refrigerate for 12 hours before serving.

Makes 12 to 16 portions.

Rhubarb and Strawberry Pie with Pastry Hearts

s all-purpose flour	500 mL
grated orange peel	5 mL
salt	2 mL
ps unsalted butter, ed	300 mL
cup ice water	50 to 75 mL
ranulated sugar	250 mL
inute tapioca	25 mL
rnstarch	10 mL
t	1 mL
tmeg	1 mL
chopped pink b, in 1-inch) chunks	875 mL
sh orange juice	50 mL
coarsely sliced, d strawberries	375 mL
salted butter	15 mL

At La Cachette in Vancouver, chef-owner Barbara Gordon makes dozens of these pies when rhubarb becomes available in the spring. Toronto readers who discovered the recipe in my column "Canadian Cookbook" tell me it's become a spring ritual for them too.

In a large bowl, combine flour, orange peel and salt. With pastry blender or 2 knives, cut in the butter until mixture looks like rolled oats. Sprinkle with water while stirring and pressing the ingredients to form a dough. Shape into 2 balls and flatten; wrap and chill while preparing the filling.

FILLING: In a large bowl, blend together sugar, tapioca, cornstarch, salt and nutmeg. Prepare the rhubarb, orange juice and strawberries and set each aside.

Roll out half the dough and line a deep 10-inch (1.5 L) pie plate. Trim the pastry about ½ inch (1 cm) from the rim; fold under neatly and flute. Roll out the remaining dough and cut out twenty-four 2½-inch (6 cm) hearts and set aside (other shapes, of course, do not affect the taste of the pie, but the hearts make it authentic La Cachette).

Toss rhubarb in the sugar mixture; stir in the orange juice and spoon mixture evenly into the lined pie plate. Scatter strawberries over top and dot with butter. Place hearts in a random fashion over the top of the pie.

Bake at 450°F (230°C) for 10 minutes. Reduce heat to 350°F (180°C) and continue baking for 30 to 35 minutes longer or until the pastry is golden and the filling bubbly. Because rhubarb and strawberries are both juicy, lay a sheet of aluminum foil in the bottom of the oven to catch any drips.

Let pie cool on a rack. Cut into 8 to 10 wedges and serve with a scoop of the best vanilla ice cream.

Blueberry Lemon Cream Pie

This pie is always outstanding among the sweets Hamiltonian Jean McKay sets out for a buffet party. With its crisp buttery crust, creamy lemon custard studded with fresh blueberries, rich blueberry glaze and garnish of whipped cream, this is a sinfully good pie.

PASTRY:

1½ cups cake and pastry flour	375 mL
4 tsp granulated sugar	20 mL
¼ tsp salt	1 mL
½ cup cold butter	125 mL
2 tbsp (approx) ice water	25 mL

FILLING:

½ envelope unflavoured gelatin	½
2 tbsp cold water	25 mL
1 egg, separated	1
¼ cup granulated sugar	50 mL
¼ tsp salt	1 mL
¼ cup lemon juice	50 mL
½ cup cream cheese (4 oz/125 g)	125 mL
3 tbsp icing sugar	50 mL
1½ cups blueberries	375 mL

GLAZE:

2 cups blueberries	500 mL
¾ cup granulated sugar	175 mL
¼ cup water	50 mL
2 tbsp cornstarch	25 mL
2 tbsp cold water	25 mL

GARNISH:

¾ cup whipping cream	175 mL
5 perfect blueberries	5
Mint leaves	

PASTRY: Mix together flour, sugar and salt in a bowl. With pastry blender or 2 knives, cut in the butter. Sprinkle with ice water, tossing to distribute the moisture, then pressing together to form a ball. Add more water if necessary. With lightly floured hands, place the dough on a sheet of waxed paper and form it into a disk about 5 inches (12 cm) in diameter. Wrap and chill for 30 minutes.

Unwrap but leave the pastry in the middle of the waxed paper. Cover with a second sheet of waxed paper and roll out to about 11 inches (28 cm) in diameter. Peel off the top layer of paper and invert the pastry onto a deep 9-inch (1 L) pie plate. Peel off the remaining paper and ease the pastry into the plate. Trim the edges and flute neatly. (Rolling the pastry in waxed paper makes this delicate pastry easier to handle.) Chill the prepared pie shell for 20 minutes.

Line the pie shell with foil and fill with dried beans or rice. Bake at 450°F (230°C) for 10 minutes. Remove the foil and beans (reserve the beans and re-use whenever making a pie shell). Prick the bottom and sides of the pastry with a fork. To prevent the edges of the pastry from browning too much, wrap them loosely with strips of foil. Return the pie to the oven for 3 to 5 minutes or until beautifully golden. Remove the foil strips and let pie shell cool on a rack. This procedure may seem like a lot of work but it ensures an evenly golden pie shell with minimum bubbling and shrinkage.

FILLING: Sprinkle gelatin over cold water and set aside to soften. Combine egg yolk, granulated sugar, salt and lemon juice in a small saucepan. Beat together and place over medium heat. Cook, stirring constantly, for about 5 minutes or until mixture is thick enough to coat a spoon. Stir in the gelatin and remove from heat.

Beat cream cheese until smooth. Blend in lemon custard and chill.

Beat egg white until soft peaks form. Continue beating while adding the icing sugar, 1 tbsp (15 mL) at a time, until firm glossy peaks form. Fold into the cooled custard and spoon into pie shell. Smooth surface and refrigerate until set, about 45 minutes. Sprinkle the blueberries over the custard and keep chilled while preparing the glaze.

GLAZE: In a small saucepan, combine blueberries, sugar and ¼ cup (50 mL) water. Cook over moderate heat for 5 minutes or until berries are tender. Remove from heat and drain, reserving the liquid.

Blend the cornstarch into 2 tbsp (25 mL) cold water and combine with blueberry liquid in small saucepan. Cook until the liquid thickens and clears, 4 to 5 minutes. Remove from heat and gently stir in the blueberries. Let cool to lukewarm. Spoon evenly over the pie and regrigerate.

At serving time, whip cream and pipe or spoon attractively over the pie. Place the berries and mint in the centre of the cream and serve.

Makes 8 servings.

Note: For Raspberry Lemon Cream Pie, substitute red, blue or black raspberries. For glaze, press cooked berries through sieve to remove seeds, if desired.

Deep-dish Blue Raspberry and Rhubarb Pie

Anita Goldberg, who teaches cooking in Trenton, Ontario, picks blue raspberries in nearby Prince Edward County for this old-fashioned deep-dish pie. The more common red berries are fine for this recipe too.

Pastry for one 9-inch (23 cm) single-crust pie	
4 cups chopped rhubarb (1 lb/500 g)	1 L
Boiling water	
2 cups blue raspberries (10 oz/300 g)	500 mL
1¼ cups granulated sugar	300 mL
¼ cup all-purpose flour	50 mL
½ tsp cinnamon	2 mL
2 tbsp butter	25 mL

Place rhubarb in a heatproof bowl. Cover with boiling water and let stand for 5 minutes. Drain well, pat dry and combine with berries in a large bowl.

Blend together sugar, flour and cinnamon. Pour over fruit and toss together lightly. Spoon evenly into a 9-inch square (2 L) cake pan. Dot with butter.

Roll out pastry to fit pan and place over fruit. Either trim or turn edges under. Press pastry to the inside of the pan around the top with the tines of a fork. Cut out a circle of pastry about the size of a nickel from the centre of the pie and insert a 2-inch (5 cm) funnel made from a strip of foil.

Bake at 400°F (200°C) for 40 minutes or until the crust is golden brown and the juices are bubbling up the funnel and around the edges.

Best served while still warm with whipped cream or ice cream. Serves 9 fruit pie-lovers.

Pear and Pistachio Strudel

Strudel used to be the preserve of cooks and bakers who were masters of the art of stretching strudel dough. While this technique is not impossible to acquire, many strudel makers happily substitute phyllo or strudel dough available in supermarkets or in grocery stores featuring Central European or Greek foods.

FILLING:

6 large, ripe, juicy but firm pears, Bartlett recommended (2½ lb/1.15 kg)	6
1 cup golden raisins	250 mL
¾ cup chopped natural pistachios (unsalted and undyed)	175 mL
¾ cup fine bread crumbs, from day-old Mediterranean-style bread	175 mL
⅔ cup granulated sugar	150 mL
¼ cup pear brandy	50 mL
1 tsp grated lemon peel	5 mL
1 tbsp lemon juice	15 mL
¼ tsp freshly grated nutmeg	1 mL

PASTRY:

1 pkg (1 lb/454 g) strudel or phyllo pastry	1
¾ cup unsalted butter, melted	175 mL

GARNISH:

2 tbsp icing sugar	25 mL
1 cup whipping cream	250 mL
2 tbsp chopped natural pistachios	25 mL

Lightly butter 2 baking sheets and set aside.

Peel, halve and core pears; dice into ¼-inch (5 mm) pieces. In a large bowl, combine diced pears, raisins, nuts, bread crumbs, sugar, pear brandy, lemon peel and juice, and nutmeg.

Cover 20 of the strudel sheets with a damp tea towel and keep covered while you work. Remove 1 sheet; place on a dry tea towel and brush lightly with melted butter and top with another strudel sheet. Brush with butter and repeat with 3 more sheets, brushing each with butter. Use 5 sheets for each strudel.

Scoop out about ¼ of the pear mixture and spread it evenly in a 2-inch (5 cm) band along one of the long sides of the layered strudel sheets. Using the towel as an aid, roll pastry one turn, just enough to enclose pear filling.

Fold in a ½-inch (1 cm) border along remaining 3 sides of strudel sheets. (These folds help to keep the filling in.) Continue rolling up strudel and place seam side down on a baking sheet. Repeat with remaining strudel sheets and filling mixture to make 3 more rolls. Place 2 filled strudels on each baking sheet.

Prick 6 steam holes on the top of each roll. Bake at 375°F (190°C) for 30 to 35 minutes or until crisp and golden brown. Transfer to a fine meshed rack.

While still warm, sprinkle each roll generously with icing sugar. Whip cream, sprinkle with chopped pistachios and serve strudel and cream immediately. To serve some of the strudel later, let it cool, wrap well in foil and freeze.

Each strudel makes 8 generous slices, 32 pieces in total. An excellent dessert for a party.

Tarte au Sucre

A memorable maple sugar pie from Quebec.

One 9-inch (1 L) unbaked pie shell

FILLING:

¾ cup water	175 mL
1¾ cups grated or granular maple sugar	425 mL
1 cup whipping cream	250 mL
½ cup light cream	125 mL
⅓ cup butter	75 mL
⅓ cup all-purpose flour	75 mL
½ cup coarsely chopped walnuts	125 mL

GARNISH:

1 cup whipping cream	250 mL

For the filling, combine water and sugar in a saucepan and bring to a boil, uncovered, over medium heat. Reduce heat and simmer for 5 minutes. Heat whipping and light cream and add to the syrup. Simmer for 5 minutes longer. Don't be alarmed if the mixture separates slightly.

Meanwhile, melt butter. Blend in flour and cook, stirring almost constantly, until thickened and smooth but not brown. Whisk a big spoonful at a time into the sugar mixture and cook, whisking gently, until evenly thickened and smooth, 2 to 3 minutes. Refrigerate until completely cool.

Sprinkle the walnuts into the pie shell and spoon in the filling. Bake at 450°F (230°C) for 10 minutes. Reduce heat to 350°F (180°C) and bake for 20 to 25 minutes longer or until the pastry is golden.

Let pie cool on a rack. Whip cream and pipe or spoon over the pie.

Makes 6 to 8 servings.

Faye Peters' Prize Peanut Pie

Faye Peters of Simcoe, Ontario, won first prize at the county fair for this pie. The peanuts she uses are grown at Windham Centre, just north of Simcoe.

One 9-inch (1 L) unbaked pie shell

FILLING:

3 eggs	3
½ cup firmly packed light brown sugar	125 mL
Pinch salt	Pinch
1 cup light corn syrup	250 mL
3 tbsp butter	50 mL
1½ tsp vanilla	7 mL

In a large saucepan, beat eggs and mix in brown sugar, salt, corn syrup, butter and vanilla. Warm over low heat just until the butter melts. Remove from heat.

Chop ¾ cup (175 mL) of the peanuts for the filling and break the remainder into halves. Mix the chopped nuts with the flour and then stir into the batter. Pour into the pie

1 cup shelled, skinned, unsalted peanuts	250 mL
1 tbsp flour	15 mL

GARNISH:

1 cup whipping cream	250 mL
$\frac{1}{4}$ cup shelled, skinned, unsalted peanuts, chopped	50 mL

shell and sprinkle the halved peanuts over the surface.

Bake at 350°F (180°C) for 40 minutes or until a toothpick inserted into the middle comes out clean. Remove from the oven and let cool.

To serve, whip cream and pipe or spoon decoratively around the pie. Sprinkle the cream with the garnishing peanuts.

Since this pie is so rich, cut into 8 small pieces.

Maple Syrup Shoofly Pie

This is one of the best-known Mennonite pies, and a big seller in Waterloo County restaurants and markets. The recipe calls for maple syrup but a stronger-flavoured version uses molasses or a molasses and corn syrup combination. In any event, this is a rich pie; I like to serve it in small wedges with unsweetened whipped cream, lightly flavoured with vanilla and nutmeg.

One 10-inch (1.5 L) unpricked, unbaked pie shell

FILLING:

1 cup maple syrup	250 mL
$\frac{3}{4}$ cup cold water	175 mL
$\frac{3}{4}$ tsp soda	4 mL
$\frac{1}{4}$ cup hot water	50 mL
1 cup cake and pastry [illegible]	250 mL
[illegible]	[illegible]

GARNISH:

1 cup whipping cream	250 mL
$\frac{1}{2}$ tsp vanilla	2 mL
Pinch freshly grated nutmeg	Pinch

Pour maple syrup and cold water into a medium bowl. Dissolve soda in the hot water and add to the syrup mixture.

Combine flour, brown sugar and salt. Work in the butter, [illegible] fingertips. Measure and reserve $\frac{2}{3}$ cup (150 mL) [illegible] mix the remaining crumbs into the syrup [illegible] into the pie shell and sprinkle [illegible] the top.

[illegible] Reduce heat to 325°F [illegible] or until the filling is [illegible] is a beautiful bronze.

Whip the cream [illegible] nutmeg. Pass whipped cream in a [illegible]

Makes 8 to 10 servings.

Classic Mincemeat Pie

Flaky pastry for a double-crust 9-inch (1 L) pie	
4 cups Burwick House Mincemeat (recipe follows)	1 L
1 egg yolk	1
1 tsp water	5 mL
2 tsp granulated sugar	10 mL

Flaky pastry suits mincemeat best, and an egg and sugar glaze gives the pie a professional touch.

Line pie plate with pastry but do not trim. Fill with mincemeat. Moisten the rim of the pastry with water and cover with the top layer of pastry. Gently press the layers together along the rim. Trim bottom pastry ½ inch (1 cm) from the edge of the pie plate; fold the overhang up over the rim and crimp the edges together. This double fold should keep all the juices inside.

Combine egg yolk and water and brush over the top of the pie. Sprinkle with sugar. Slash a decorative pattern for steam holes. Bake at 450°F (230°C) for 15 minutes. Reduce heat to 350°F (180°C) and bake for 30 minutes longer or until pastry is golden and filling bubbly.

Serve warm with whipped cream or ice cream.

Makes 6 to 8 servings.

Burwick House Mincemeat

3 lemons	3
8 medium apples (2¾ lb/1.275 kg total)	8
4 cups firmly packed brown sugar	1 L
2½ cups currants (12 oz/375 g)	625 mL
2½ cups seedless raisins (12 oz/375 g)	625 mL
2 cups finely grated suet (6 oz/175 g)	500 mL
½ cup chopped mixed candied peel (4 oz/125 g)	125 mL

Burwick is the name of one of the houses at Black Creek Pioneer Village in northwest Metropolitan Toronto. This mincemeat, which well-off families at the time of Confederation would have made, is prepared in the kitchen of the house for visitors to sample. The more exotic ingredients, such as the spices, lemons, currants and raisins, were becoming more available in Canada in the 1860s, while the apples, suet and cider were more than likely homegrown and homemade.

Grate lemons and squeeze out their juice. Peel, core and grate apples coarsely to make 8 cups (2 L). Mix lemon peel, juice, apples and all the remaining ingredients except the apple cider in a large bowl. (At this stage the mincemeat

1 tsp freshly grated nutmeg	5 mL
½ tsp cinnamon	2 mL
¼ tsp cloves	1 mL
¼ tsp salt	1 mL
2 tbsp brandy	25 mL
Apple cider or apple juice	

is quite runny, but within 2 days the dried fruit will have absorbed most of the liquid.)

In the 1860s, the cook then transferred the mincemeat to a crock with a close fitting lid, and left it to ripen in a cool pantry or fruit cellar for 2 weeks. I have good results storing the mincemeat in a covered plastic container in the refrigerator. Add cider if the mincemeat is too dry or more dried fruit if too moist. I find that the recipe has just the right moistness, but it might be important to note that I use juicy McIntosh apples. Stir the mincemeat from time to time, but no excessive tasting or there won't be enough for pies.

Makes 11 cups (2.75 L), enough for 2 pies and a few tarts.

Old-fashioned Fruit and Nut Bars

½ cup butter	125 mL
1 cup granulated sugar	250 mL
2 eggs	2
1 tsp vanilla	5 mL
⅔ cup unbleached or regular all-purpose flour	150 mL
1 tsp baking powder	5 mL
Pinch salt	Pinch
2 cups finely chopped dates	500 mL
1 cup chopped pecans or freshly shelled walnuts	250 mL
½ cup candied cherries	125 mL
Icing sugar	

Dates, cherries and pecans give these bars a moist chewiness and flavour that improves with a day's aging.

Grease a 9-inch square (2.5 L) cake pan and set aside.

In a large bowl, cream together butter and granulated sugar. Beat in the eggs, one at a time, and the vanilla.

Stir together flour, baking powder and salt and sprinkle over the batter. Place dates, nuts and cherries on top of dry ingredients and stir together briefly just until blended.

Transfer batter to prepared pan. Smooth surface and bake at 350°F (180°C) for 40 to 45 minutes or until a skewer inserted into the middle comes out clean. Let cool in the pan, then cut into bars. Sprinkle with icing sugar and serve.

Makes about 25 bars.

Apricot and Fig Almond Bars

1 cup chopped dried apricots	250 mL
¼ cup water	50 mL

SHORTBREAD BASE:

½ cup butter, softened	125 mL
¼ cup granulated sugar	50 mL
1 cup all-purpose flour	250 mL

TOPPING:

2 eggs	2
1 cup firmly packed brown sugar	250 mL
1 tsp vanilla	5 mL
⅓ cup all-purpose flour	75 mL
½ tsp baking powder	2 mL
¼ tsp salt	1 mL
½ cup chopped almonds (blanched or unblanched)	125 mL
¼ cup chopped dried figs	50 mL
1 tsp grated orange peel	5 mL
2 tbsp icing sugar	25 mL

Apricot is one of the most beguiling of fruit flavours. It has tang and intensity. Apricots with figs and almonds in a brown sugar-egg batter form a rich layer over a buttery shortbread. These bars keep and freeze well, and are particularly pretty served in little pleated paper cups. They also make good additions to the daily brown bag.

Grease a 9-inch square (2.5 L) cake pan and set aside

Combine the apricots and water in a small saucepan. Cover tightly and bring to a boil; reduce heat to the lowest setting and simmer gently for 10 minutes or until apricots are tender but not mushy. Drain any excess water and let cool.

SHORTBREAD BASE: Cream together butter and sugar. Mix in the flour and pat into prepared pan. Bake at 350°F (180°C) for 12 to 15 minutes or until pale gold in colour.

TOPPING: Beat together the eggs, brown sugar and vanilla. Mix together the flour, baking powder and salt and stir into the batter along with the almonds, figs and orange peel.

Pour the topping over the shortbread base. Bake at 350°F (180°C) for 30 to 35 minutes or until medium-brown. Let cool and store in airtight containers.

To serve, cut into bars and sprinkle with icing sugar.

Makes 24 bars.

Walnut Applesauce Brownies

⅓ cup butter	75 mL
1 cup firmly packed brown sugar	250 mL
1 egg	1
½ cup unsweetened applesauce	125 mL
1 tbsp coarsely grated orange peel	15 mL
½ tsp vanilla	2 mL
1¼ cups all-purpose flour	300 mL
1 tsp baking powder	5 mL
¼ tsp soda	1 mL
¼ tsp salt	1 mL
½ cup chopped, freshly shelled walnuts	125 mL
½ cup finely chopped dates	125 mL
2 tbsp wheat germ	25 mL

ICING:

1 cup icing sugar	250 mL
5 tsp orange juice	25 mL
½ tsp vanilla	2 mL

This recipe is adapted from one in *Apple Recipes*, a cookbook compiled by the women's group of Grace United Church, Thornbury, Ontario, to mark the church's centennial in 1980.

You will search in vain for chocolate in these "brownies." They are more like a fruit and nut square with a hint of orange. They freeze and keep well.

Grease a 13 x 9-inch (4 L) cake pan and set aside.

Combine butter and brown sugar in a saucepan and heat gently until butter is melted. Transfer to a large bowl and let cool.

Beat in egg, applesauce, orange peel and vanilla. In a second bowl, stir together flour, baking powder, soda and salt. Add walnuts, dates and wheat germ and toss together, separating the date pieces. Add to butter mixture and stir just until blended.

Spread batter evenly in prepared pan and bake at 350°F (180°C) for 20 to 25 minutes or until centre of cake springs back when lightly touched and the cake has shrunk away from the sides of the pan. Remove from the oven and let cool for 5 minutes.

ICING: Sift icing sugar into a bowl. Mix in orange juice and vanilla and spread evenly and quickly onto cake. Note the icing is more like a thin glaze than a thick icing and that it firms up quickly on the cake. No dallying once you've begun to spread. Let cool, cover and store brownies in the pan.

Makes 24 squares.

Ginger Shortbread Fingers

1 lb butter	454 g
1 cup super fine granulated sugar	250 mL
1 cup rice flour	250 mL
3 cups all-purpose flour	750 mL
¾ tsp ground ginger	4 mL
2 tbsp finely chopped preserved ginger	25 mL
2 tbsp granulated sugar	25 mL

A basic shortbread takes on gingery highlights. This is an adaptation of Anne Lindsay McColl's grandmother's recipe.

Set out a 15 x 10-inch (2 L) jelly roll pan.

In a large bowl, cream together butter and super fine sugar. Gradually add rice flour, all-purpose flour and ground ginger. As mixture stiffens, work ingredients together by hand and knead for 5 minutes or until shortbread is very smooth. Mix in chopped ginger.

Pat dough into jelly roll pan and score into 32 fingers with a knife. Prick shortbread in symmetrical rows with a fork. Sprinkle with granulated sugar.

Bake at 350°F (180°C) for 10 minutes. Reduce heat to 300°F (150°C) and bake for 40 minutes longer or until golden. Cut along scored lines. Let cool, remove from pan and store in airtight containers. Cookies will keep well for up to 2 weeks.

Makes 32 fingers.

Pecan Balls

1½ cups all-purpose flour	375 mL
½ cup ground pecans	125 mL
¼ cup granulated sugar	50 mL
¼ tsp salt	1 mL
¾ cup unsalted butter	175 mL
½ tsp vanilla	2 mL
½ cup icing sugar	125 mL

Nutty buttery balls are a good make-ahead cookie, and go well with fruit sherbets, fresh fruit and afternoon tea.

Grease 2 baking sheets and set aside.

In a large bowl, combine flour, pecans, granulated sugar and salt. Work in butter and vanilla, first with a pastry blender, then by hand to make a smooth dough.

Form dough into 1-inch (2.5 cm) balls and transfer to baking sheets. Bake at 300°F (150°C) for 20 to 25 minutes or until firm and lightly browned on the bottom.

While still hot, roll balls in icing sugar and let cool on a rack. Reserve leftover icing sugar. Store cookies in a covered container. Before serving, sieve remaining icing sugar over top of the balls.

Makes 36 balls.

Whisky Walnut Snaps

1 cup all-purpose flour	250 mL
¼ tsp salt	1 mL
1 cup chopped, freshly shelled walnuts	250 mL
½ cup corn syrup	125 mL
½ cup unsalted butter	125 mL
⅔ cup firmly packed brown sugar	150 mL
2 tsp whisky	10 mL

Fine lacy rounds add an elegant touch to after-dinner coffee or afternoon tea.

Grease 2 baking sheets and set aside.

In a bowl, combine flour, salt and nuts and set aside.

In a medium saucepan, combine corn syrup, butter and brown sugar and bring to a boil. Remove from heat and immediately blend in floured nuts and whisky.

Drop batter by the teaspoonful (5 mL) onto baking sheets, leaving 3 inches (7 cm) between cookies. Bake at 325°F (160°C) for 6 to 8 minutes or until cookies spread and have a caramel-brown, cratered surface.

Remove from the oven and let cool for 1 minute on baking sheets. Transfer to racks to cool and stiffen. Store in airtight containers.

Makes about 60 cookies.

Lord Dufferin Spice and Molasses Crinkles

¾ cup shortening	175 mL
1 cup firmly packed brown sugar	250 mL
1 egg	1
¼ cup molasses	50 mL
1¾ cups all-purpose flour	425 mL
2 tsp soda	10 mL
1 tsp each cinnamon and ginger	5 mL
½ tsp ground cloves	2 mL
¼ tsp salt	1 mL
Granulated sugar	
Water	

This is an 1830s no-roll version of the ever-popular crunchy gingerbread. The pupils at Lord Dufferin School loved making these cookies for their school's centennial in 1976.

Grease 2 baking sheets and set aside.

Cream together shortening and brown sugar. Mix in the egg and molasses. Stir together flour, soda, cinnamon, ginger, cloves and salt. Blend into molasses mixture.

Form dough into 1¼-inch (3 cm) balls. Flatten each ball slightly and dip the top into granulated sugar. Place the balls, sugared side up, about 2 inches (5 cm) apart on baking sheets. Sprinkle each ball with 2 drops of water.

Bake at 375°F (190°C) for 10 to 12 minutes or until very crinkly and set but not hard. Carefully remove from baking sheets and let cool on racks. Store in airtight containers.

Makes about 60 crinkles.

Coconut Oatmeal Crisps

1 cup shortening	250 mL
1 cup granulated sugar	250 mL
½ cup firmly packed brown sugar	125 mL
2 eggs	2
1 tsp vanilla	5 mL
1¼ cups regular rolled oats	300 mL
¾ cup desiccated coconut	175 mL
1½ cups all-purpose flour	375 mL
1 tsp baking powder	5 mL
1 tsp soda	5 mL
½ tsp salt	2 mL
Granulated sugar	

Over the years my mother-in-law, Gertrude Baird, made thousands of cookies for children, grandchildren, neighbours and friends. These coconut oatmeal crisps have remained family favourites for three generations.

Grease 2 baking sheets and set aside.

Cream together shortening and both kinds of sugar; beat in the eggs, vanilla, oats and coconut.

Stir together flour, baking powder, soda and salt. Blend into batter to form a fairly stiff dough.

Place teaspoonsful (5 mL) of dough about 2 inches (5 cm) apart on baking sheets. Flatten each cookie with a fork, dipping the fork into granulated sugar to keep it from sticking.

Bake at 350°F (180°C) for 8 to 10 minutes or until firm but still light coloured. Let cool on racks and store in airtight containers.

Makes about 72 crisps.

Aulets

½ cup lard	125 mL
½ cup butter	125 mL
1 cup granulated sugar	250 mL
1 tsp vanilla	5 mL
1 egg	1
4 tsp white vinegar	20 mL
2½ cups all-purpose flour	625 mL
1 tsp soda	5 mL
½ tsp freshly grated nutmeg	2 mL
¼ tsp salt	1 mL

GARNISH:

Raisins, small candies or coarse granulated sugar

In Acadian tradition, these specially shaped sugar cookies were given to one's godchildren at Christmas. Jacqueline Thibault of Comeauville, Nova Scotia, remembers aulets shaped like gingerbread men, with raisins or small candies for the eyes, nose and mouth: "The larger the aulet, the better. It was not touched on Christmas Day because you kept it for a few days to show your friends and compare it with theirs."

Lightly grease 2 baking sheets and set aside.

In a large bowl, cream together lard, butter, sugar and vanilla until light and fluffy. Beat in the egg and vinegar.

Mix together flour, soda, nutmeg and salt and blend into the batter. Form the dough into 3 smooth balls. (Cover and chill if not rolling out immediately. Bring dough back to room temperature before proceeding.)

On a lightly floured counter or pastry cloth, roll out each portion of dough to slightly less than ¼-inch (5 mm) thickness and cut into shapes. Use a gingerbread cutter for authentic aulet, but the cookies taste just as good in other seasonal shapes, even circles. Decorate with raisins or candies or sprinkle with sugar. Transfer carefully to baking sheets.

Bake at 375° F (190° C) for 8 to 10 minutes or until golden underneath. Pay careful attention while the cookies are baking, turning the baking sheets around on the racks and switching top to bottom so the cookies brown evenly without burning.

Makes about 36 aulets or 48 two-inch (5 cm) cookies.

Maple Mousse

2 envelopes unflavoured gelatin	2
¼ cup water	50 mL
1½ cups maple syrup	375 mL
4 eggs, separated	4
¼ cup maple liqueur	50 mL
2 cups whipping cream	500 mL
¾ cup sliced almonds	175 mL

This creamy maple custard pudding is as old as fine dining in Canada, and has regained the affection of cooks in the last decade.

In a small bowl, stir gelatin into the water and let stand to soften.

In the top of a double boiler, combine maple syrup and egg yolks. Stirring constantly, cook until slightly thickened and clear, about 8 minutes. Remove from heat. Add softened gelatin and stir until gelatin has dissolved. Stir in liqueur, let cool and chill until custard thickens and has the consistency of raw egg whites, about 45 minutes.

In a large bowl, beat egg whites until stiff but not dry peaks form. Whip the cream and fold first the cream, then the egg whites into the custard. Transfer mousse to a 6-cup (1.5 L) glass or crystal serving dish, cover and chill for 3 to 4 hours or overnight.

Spread almonds in a single layer in a cake pan and toast at 350° F (180° C) until golden brown, 5 to 8 minutes, stirring once or twice. Let cool and set aside.

To serve, sprinkle almonds in a ring around the outside edge of dish. A dollop of whipped cream is not amiss with the mousse.

Makes 8 servings.

Seedless Raspberry Mousse with Crème Anglaise

5 cups raspberries (red, blue or black)	1.25 L
½ cup water	125 mL
1 envelope unflavoured gelatin	1
⅔ cup granulated sugar	150 mL
2 tbsp lemon juice	25 mL
1 tbsp kirsch or framboise (optional but recommended)	15 mL
Pinch salt	Pinch
3 egg whites	3
1 cup whipping cream	250 mL

CRÈME ANGLAISE:

1½ cups milk	375 mL
3 egg yolks	3
3 tbsp granulated sugar	50 mL
½ tsp vanilla	2 mL

Mousse desserts are an elegant improvement on that old standby: fruit and cream.

Reserve about ½ cup (125 mL) raspberries for garnish. Purée remaining berries in a food mill or crush and press through a sieve into a large bowl. Refrigerate purée and swish seeds with water to extract all their flavour. Strain liquid into a small saucepan and discard seeds.

Stir gelatin and ½ cup (125 mL) of the sugar into the liquid. Heat gently over medium heat until gelatin and sugar have dissolved and liquid is syrupy. Remove from heat. Add lemon juice, kirsch if using, and salt. Blend into purée and refrigerate until thickened to the consistency of unbeaten egg whites.

Beat egg whites at high speed until soft peaks form. Continue beating, adding remaining sugar, until peaks are firm and glossy. Whip cream and fold into raspberry mixture. Stir in about ¼ of the egg whites, then fold in the remainder. Transfer to an 8-cup (2 L) bowl (an old-fashioned glass compote is pretty but any plain container will look attractive). Cover and refrigerate until firm, about 4 hours.

CREME ANGLAISE: Scald milk in the top of a double boiler (bubbles form around edges of pan). Beat together egg yolks and sugar. Stir about ½ cup (125 mL) of hot milk into the yolks, then pour into the saucepan. Set over simmering water. Stirring constantly but gently, cook custard until thick enough to coat a wooden spoon. Remove from heat and strain. Add vanilla and pour into a pitcher to cool. To prevent a skin from forming on the surface of the custard, float a little cream or milk on top. Cover and chill. Stir just before serving.

To serve, top mousse with reserved berries. Spoon into individual dishes and top with Crème Anglaise.

Makes 6 very generous portions.

Tangerine Sherbet

1 cup granulated sugar	250 mL
1 cup water	250 mL
1 tsp grated orange peel	5 mL
1 tsp grated lemon peel	5 mL
1¾ cups tangerine juice	425 mL
½ cup lemon juice	125 mL
Scented geranium leaves or mint	

Start a new Christmas tradition in your house — serve a tangy sherbet instead of pudding.

In a medium saucepan, combine sugar and water. Heat, stirring, until sugar dissolves. Increase heat and simmer for 5 minutes. Let cool.

Mix together syrup, orange and lemon peel, and tangerine and lemon juice. Freeze in an ice-cream machine according to manufacturer's instructions. Or pour into a flat cake pan and freeze until almost solid. Break into large chunks and in a chilled bowl, beat with an electric mixer until a beautiful pale, opaque orange. (Quick results can be had by puréeing chunks in a food processor or blender.) Transfer to airtight containers and freeze until firm but not hard.

Serve sherbet in large scoops garnished with scented geranium leaves or mint.

Makes 6 servings, about ½ cup (125 mL) each.

Maple Ice Cream with Toasted Hazelnut Praline

2 cups whipping cream	500 mL
1⅓ cups maple syrup	325 mL
⅔ cup milk	150 mL
⅓ cup maple liqueur	75 mL

TOASTED HAZELNUT PRALINE:

½ cup hazelnuts	125 mL
½ cup granulated sugar	125 mL
2 tbsp water	25 mL

Maple liqueur accentuates the creamy flavour of this old-fashioned churned ice cream. For a touch of class and a welcome crunch, nothing beats a sprinkling of toasted hazelnut praline.

In a large bowl, combine cream, syrup, milk and liqueur. Pour into canister of churn freezer or into ice-cream machine and freeze according to manufacturer's instructions. For soft ice cream, serve immediately with a sprinkle of praline. Or scrape into airtight containers and store in the freezer until needed. Fifteen minutes before serving, transfer to refrigerator to soften for easy scooping.

TOASTED HAZELNUT PRALINE: Place hazelnuts in a single layer in a medium cake pan and toast at 350° F (180° C) for 10 minutes or until skins crack to reveal toasty golden nutmeats. Immediately rub hazelnuts vigorously in a terry kitchen towel to remove most of the dark brown skins. Don't worry about a few pieces that stick to the nuts.

In a small heavy saucepan, mix together sugar and water. Bring to a boil over high heat and cook until caramel coloured, 4 to 5 minutes. Add nuts, bring back to a boil and immediately pour into cake pan. Let cool completely. Break praline into large chunks and pulverize in a food processor or blender or with a mallet. Store in an airtight container at room temperature for up to a month.

To serve, scoop ice cream into chilled bowls or stemmed glasses and top with a sprinkle of hazelnut praline.

Makes 6 generous servings.

Skyr

16 cups buttermilk	4 L
1 cup whipping cream	250 mL
¾ cup light cream	175 mL
⅓ cup granulated sugar	75 mL

Karla Thomson, who is originally from Gimli, a Manitoba town founded by Icelandic settlers, calls this thick baked buttermilk sauce "Icelandic ice cream". This is adapted from her grandmother's recipe.

Pour buttermilk into 2 large ovenproof bowls and bake, uncovered, at 200° F (100° C) for 4 hours.

Line a large colander with fine cheesecloth and place in the sink. Pour in baked buttermilk and let clear liquid drain for 1¼ hours.

Transfer thick sauce to a food processor and process with whipping and light creams and sugar until silky smooth. Or combine the ingredients in a large bowl and beat until smooth and light. Karla Thomson's grandmother used to do this by hand, and it took her considerably longer than it will take us with our various electric machines. Refrigerate until serving time.

Makes 5 cups (1.25 L).

Bungees' Wild Rice and Blueberry Pudding

1/4 cup wild rice	50 mL
1/3 cup water	75 mL
1/2 cup raisins	125 mL
4 cups milk	1 L
1 cup granulated sugar	250 mL
6 eggs	6
1 tsp vanilla	5 mL

SAUCE:

2 cups blueberries, wild recommended	500 mL
1/2 cup granulated sugar	125 mL

This pudding combines two of Manitoba's best products—wild rice and blueberries. The recipe originated at Bungees (now The Teepee), a Saulteaux Indian restaurant in downtown Winnipeg.

Lightly butter the bottoms of 10 custard cups.

Rinse rice and combine with water in a small saucepan. Cover and bring to a boil. Reduce heat and cook over low heat for 15 to 20 minutes or until tender but not mushy. Drain well and mix with the raisins. Divide equally among the custard cups.

In a saucepan, combine milk and sugar and bring to a simmer. Remove from heat. Beat eggs, blend in some of the hot milk, then stirring constantly, pour mixture into the pan. Add the vanilla and gently pour over the rice and raisins.

Set the individual cups in a large shallow pan or pans. Pour enough boiling water into the pan to come halfway up the sides of the cups. Bake at 325° F (160° C) for 40 to 45 minutes or until the tip of a sharp knife inserted into the middle of the custard comes out clean. Chill thoroughly.

SAUCE: Lightly crush half the blueberries in a saucepan. Add the remaining berries and sugar and bring to a boil, stirring constantly. Reduce heat to medium and simmer for 5 minutes or until the berries are tender. Let cool.

To serve, unmould the custard onto small plates and spoon sauce over the top.

Makes 10 servings.

Summer Pudding

4 cups raspberries	1 L
2 cups stemmed red currants	500 mL
1 cup blueberries, wild recommended	250 mL
$1\frac{1}{3}$ cups granulated sugar	325 mL
8 to 10 slices ($\frac{1}{2}$ inch/ 1 cm thick) homemade-style bread, 1 day old	8 to 10
1 cup whipping cream	250 mL

Mid-summer berries blend in an easy-to-make dessert. For years I hesitated before making summer pudding, thinking the bread would make a boring dessert. I was wrong.

Place the fruit in 3 separate bowls. Sprinkle half the sugar over the red currants and divide the remaining sugar equally between the raspberries and blueberries. Crush blueberries gently to start juices flowing; stir all fruit well and let stand for 20 minutes.

Meanwhile, trim crusts from bread and reserve for future use as bread crumbs. Use 6 or 7 slices to line completely the bottom and sides of a 4 to 5-cup (1 to 1.25 L) bowl, trimming and shaping where necessary. Reserve the bread scraps and remaining slices.

Transfer blueberries to a heavy saucepan that will accommodate all fruit and cook over medium heat for about 3 minutes or until the juices run freely. Add the currants and cook gently for 2 minutes. Add the raspberries and cook for 2 minutes. Stir gently to prevent sticking. This heating step ensures that the berries release their juices, but it's vital they retain their shape and fresh flavour.

Using a slotted spoon, half-fill the bread-lined bowl with fruit. Place a single layer of bread over the fruit (use some of the scraps here if necessary) and then fill the bowl with remaining fruit and some of the juice. Shape remaining bread slices to cover fruit completely. Pour in enough juice to saturate the bread. Refrigerate the rest of the juice, if any. Place bowl on a large plate and set a small plate inside the bowl right on top of the bread. Weight down with a heavy can. Chill for 12 hours or up to 2 days.

To serve, unmould pudding onto a rimmed serving dish. Pour any reserved juices around the base of the pudding. Whip the cream and serve with neat wedges of the pudding. Serves 8 lucky summer diners.

Honey Hazelnut Baked Apples with Rum Sauce

⅓ cup golden raisins	75 mL	
⅔ cup rum	150 mL	
½ cup hazelnuts	125 mL	
¼ cup firmly packed brown sugar	50 mL	
6 large apples	6	
½ cup mild liquid honey	125 mL	
2 tbsp butter, melted	25 mL	

Northern Spy, Ida Red and Rome Beauty hold their shape well when baked. Serve these apples in your best ceramic bowls or large handsome wine goblets, and offer a bowl of unsweetened whipped cream.

Combine the raisins and rum in a measuring cup. Cover and soak for 30 minutes.

Spread the hazelnuts on a baking sheet and bake at 350°F (180°C) for 10 minutes. Rub in a terrycloth towel to remove as much of the skins as possible. Let cool and chop medium-fine by hand or with a food processor.

Using a slotted spoon, transfer the raisins to a small bowl, reserving the rum. Mix raisins, hazelnuts and brown sugar.

Wash apples and cut out a generous core, leaving ½ inch (1 cm) intact on the bottom. Make a shallow cut around the middle of the apples to let them expand as they bake. Pack the cavities with the toasted hazelnut mixture, heaping any excess on top. Place in a 11 x 7-inch (1.75 L) baking dish.

Combine the rum, honey and butter and ladle about a third of it over the apples. Bake at 350°F (180°C) for 50 to 60 minutes or until the apples are tender, basting the apples two more times with the rest of the rum sauce.

Serve hot, warm or at room temperature. Makes 6 generous and rich servings.

Nancy Phillips' Christmas Carrot Pudding

1 cup finely chopped suet	250 mL
1 cup firmly packed brown sugar	250 mL
1 cup grated raw carrots (2 medium)	250 mL
1 cup grated raw potatoes (2 medium)	250 mL
1 cup seeded raisins	250 mL
1 cup currants	250 mL
⅔ cup chopped mixed peel	150 mL
⅔ cup chopped candied cherries	150 mL
¼ cup slivered blanched almonds	50 mL
3 tbsp brandy	50 mL
1½ cups all-purpose flour	375 mL
1 tsp soda	5 mL
½ tsp salt	2 mL
1½ tsp cinnamon	7 mL
½ tsp cloves	2 mL
½ tsp freshly grated nutmeg	2 mL

From the Centennial Museum Archives in Nanaimo, British Columbia, comes this tried and true local recipe. The Phillips family have been making this pudding every Christmas for more than 90 years. You can make it six weeks before Christmas.

Grease a 6-cup (1.5 L) heatproof pudding bowl or mould. Cut out a disk of waxed paper to fit the bottom and another to fit inside the top edge. Butter both disks and place the smaller one butter side up in the bottom of the bowl. Set the larger disk aside.

In a large bowl, combine the suet, sugar, carrots, potatoes, raisins, currants, peel, cherries, almonds and brandy. Sift together flour, soda, salt and spices. Pour over fruit mixture and stir to blend all ingredients evenly.

Pack mixture firmly into pudding bowl. Cover pudding with buttered disk of waxed paper. Cut a round of foil large enough to fit over the top of the bowl and extend 2 inches (5 cm) down side of dish. Tie foil firmly with kitchen string and fold foil up over string.

Set bowl on a rack in a large saucepan. Pour in enough boiling water to come ⅔ up the sides of the bowl. Cover and bring the water to a boil. Adjust heat so water simmers vigorously around the pudding. Steam for 4 hours or until pudding has risen, is firm to the touch and gives off the fragrance of spices and fruit. Add more boiling water when necessary during cooking.

Remove bowl from saucepan and let cool. Wrap and keep chilled. To serve, resteam for 1 to 1½ hours or until heated and soft all the way to the centre. Unmould onto warmed serving plate and decorate with holly.

Serve with hard sauce, caramel sauce or custard sauce. Makes 10 servings.

QUICK BREADS AND YEAST BREADS

Pioneer bakers had their work cut out for them. They had to produce every crumb of bread consumed in the household. In winter, that meant working with unreliable yeast, and once over that hurdle, wrapping the bread in overcoats to keep it warm enough to rise overnight. The next day the youngsters in the family had to restock the woodbox to keep up with the day's baking.

What a difference today — when we make bread out of pleasure, not necessity. Still, holidays like Christmas and Easter reveal that traditional recipes for bread — such as Macedonian kosuniak and Italian cazuppa — are in no danger of disappearing. They are more than just bread; they reaffirm cultural roots at times of the year when families are closest.

Quick breads — the spicy orange squash loaf, applesauce muffins, sweet raisin scones and molasses doughnuts — are a much faster and less labour-intensive way of keeping our bread-baking skills alive. Muffins especially answer the need for something homemade, good and quick. They are popular with junior and senior cooks of both sexes, and make fine breakfast, brunch, lunch and snack fare.

Carrot Apricot Muffins

These spicy golden muffins are good for breakfasts and snacks.

1½ cups all-purpose flour	375 mL
¾ cup firmly packed brown sugar	175 mL
1 tsp baking powder	5 mL
1 tsp soda	5 mL
½ tsp salt	2 mL
½ tsp cinnamon	2 mL
¼ tsp freshly grated nutmeg	1 mL

Grease or line 12 large muffin cups and set aside.

Combine flour, sugar, baking powder, soda, salt, cinnamon, nutmeg and cloves in a large bowl. Stir to blend all ingredients.

In a smaller bowl, whisk together egg, yogurt, butter and vanilla; pour over dry ingredients. Sprinkle on carrots,

Pinch cloves	Pinch
1 egg	1
1 cup natural yogurt	250 mL
⅓ cup butter, melted	75 mL
½ tsp vanilla	2 mL
1½ cups finely grated carrots	375 mL
½ cup currants	125 mL
½ cup slivered dried apricots	125 mL
½ cup chopped pecans or freshly shelled walnuts	125 mL

currants, apricots and nuts; stir just until blended.

Transfer batter to muffin cups. Bake at 400° F (200° C) for 20 minutes or until well risen, fragrant and springy-firm to the touch.

Serve warm with unsalted butter and honey, or at room temperature with cream cheese.

Makes 12 big muffins that can be stored for up to 4 days in a covered container or frozen.

Applesauce Spice Muffins

Of all the apple muffin recipes, this is one of the lightest and tastiest. It comes from Thornbury, Ontario, in the heart of Georgian Bay apple country.

½ cup butter	125 mL
1 cup firmly packed brown sugar	250 mL
1 egg	1
1½ cups all-purpose flour	375 mL
1 tsp baking powder	5 mL
1 tsp soda	5 mL
¼ tsp salt	1 mL
¼ tsp cinnamon	1 mL
¼ tsp freshly grated nutmeg	1 mL
½ cup raisins or currants	125 mL
½ cup chopped almonds, pecans or freshly shelled walnuts	125 mL
1 cup unsweetened applesauce	250 mL

TOPPING:

2 tbsp granulated sugar	25 mL
¼ tsp cinnamon	1 mL
¼ tsp freshly grated nutmeg	1 mL

Grease or line 12 large muffin cups and set aside.

In a large bowl, cream together butter and brown sugar; beat in egg. Stir together flour, baking powder, soda, salt, cinnamon and nutmeg. Combine with raisins and almonds. Stir dry ingredients into the batter in 3 parts, alternating with the applesauce in 2 parts. Mix just until blended. Transfer to muffin cups, almost filling each cup.

TOPPING: Combine all topping ingredients and spoon equally over muffins. Bake at 375° F (190° C) for 20 minutes or until well risen and firm to the touch. Let cool on a rack and serve for breakfast or snacks.

Makes 12 big muffins.

Cornbread with Bacon

3 strips lean bacon	3
1 cup yellow cornmeal	250 mL
1 cup all-purpose flour	250 mL
1/4 cup granulated sugar	50 mL
2 tsp baking powder	10 mL
1/2 tsp soda	2 mL
1/2 tsp salt	2 mL
2 eggs	2
1 cup buttermilk	250 mL
1/3 cup butter, melted and cooled	75 mL
2/3 cup corn kernels	150 mL

Breakfast or suppertime cornbread revives the old johnny-cake tradition. Here it's improved with corn kernels and bacon.

Grease a 9-inch (2.5 L) square cake pan and set aside. Fry bacon until crisp; drain and crumble. Set aside.

In a large bowl, stir together cornmeal, flour, sugar, baking powder, soda and salt. In a smaller bowl, beat eggs and combine with buttermilk and butter. Pour over dry ingredients. Sprinkle on corn and bacon and stir together just until batter is blended and there are no dry patches.

Transfer batter to prepared pan and bake at 400° F (200° C) for 20 to 25 minutes or until well risen and bread springs back when touched in the centre. Cut into squares and serve hot.

Makes 16 pieces. Cornbread, sliced crosswise, is very pleasant toasted.

Sweet Milk Raisin Scones

2 cups all-purpose flour	500 mL
1/4 cup granulated sugar	50 mL
4 tsp baking powder	20 mL
1/2 tsp salt	2 mL
1/4 cup lard or shortening	50 mL
1/4 cup butter	50 mL
1/2 cup raisins	125 mL
1 egg	1
2/3 cup (approx) milk	150 mL

GLAZE:

1 tbsp light cream or milk	15 mL
1 tbsp granulated sugar	15 mL

Adapted from a 1909 cookbook located in the Stratford Archives, here's a recipe for scones or, as some people call them, tea biscuits. The strong Scottish presence in Stratford and vicinity for the last 150 years has guaranteed the popularity of this delicious quick bread.

Sift together flour, sugar, baking powder and salt into a large bowl. With pastry blender or 2 knives, cut in the lard and butter until mixture is crumbly. Sprinkle with raisins.

Whisk together the egg and milk. Using a fork, stir egg mixture into the dry ingredients until a soft dough forms. Add a few drops more milk if necessary.

Turn dough out onto a lightly floured counter. Knead 10

turns and divide the dough into 8 parts. Pat each portion into rounds about ¾-inch (2 cm) thick and transfer to lightly floured baking sheet. Brush with the cream and sprinkle with sugar for the glaze.

Bake at 425° F (220° C) for 18 minutes or until well risen and browned. Serve hot from the oven with butter, clover honey, strawberry jam or marmalade. Very good for breakfast, brunch or afternoon tea.

Makes enough for 6 to 8 people.

Buttermilk Bannock

1 cup whole wheat flour	250 mL
1 cup unbleached all-purpose flour	250 mL
1 tbsp baking powder	15 mL
½ tsp soda	2 mL
½ tsp salt	2 mL
¼ cup shortening	50 mL
1 cup plus 2 tbsp buttermilk	275 mL
1 tbsp whole wheat flour	15 mL

Bannocks or Scottish scones originated in the Selkirk settlement in Manitoba but are now eaten widely in the north and west. In its simplest form, a bannock is flour, water and some leavening cooked in a cast-iron frying pan over a fire in the bush. Where circumstances permit, the cook can add shortening, use milk instead of water and bake it in the oven. The version below is more luxurious.

Bannock is best when served hot as a breakfast, lunch or tea bread. Terrific with blueberry, raspberry or strawberry jam.

In a large bowl, stir together whole wheat and all-purpose flour, baking powder, soda and salt. With pastry blender or 2 knives, cut in the shortening until mixture is crumbly. Stir in the buttermilk and form into a ball.

On lightly floured surface, knead dough 8 turns. Place on a floured baking sheet and pat down into a 9-inch (23 cm) circle. Score the bannock into 8 wedges like a pie and sprinkle with the 1 tbsp (15 mL) flour. Bake at 450° F (230° C) for 15 to 18 minutes. Serve hot.

Makes 8 generous wedges.

Beignes à la Mélasse — Molasses Doughnuts

1 egg	1
½ cup granulated sugar	125 mL
½ cup molasses	125 mL
2 tbsp butter, melted	25 mL
¾ tsp soda	4 mL
½ cup buttermilk	125 mL
3¼ cups all-purpose flour	800 mL
4 tsp baking powder	20 mL
½ tsp salt	2 mL
½ tsp ginger	2 mL
¼ tsp each cinnamon and freshly grated nutmeg	1 mL
Oil for frying	
Granulated sugar for garnish	

It may be hard for modern Canadians to visualize a time when doughnuts were a seasonal treat. Among early Acadians, however, only after the fall butchering was there enough fat — either beef suet or pork lard — to make doughnuts. A big crock of them was always served with breakfast on Christmas morning. In a "waste not-want not" society, the fat was then used for pastry in the winter's supply of meat and mince pies.

In a large bowl, beat together egg, sugar, molasses and butter. Dissolve the soda in the buttermilk and stir into the batter.

Stir together flour, baking powder, salt, ginger, cinnamon and nutmeg and gradually blend into the batter to form a soft dough.

On a floured counter or pastry cloth, roll dough out to ⅓-inch (1 cm) thickness and cut into 3-inch (7 cm) circles with a doughnut cutter.

Fry in about 3 inches (7 cm) of oil heated to 360° F (185° C) for about 1½ minutes per side. Drain on paper towels and sprinkle generously with sugar while still warm.

Makes about 18 doughnuts.

Croquignoles

⅓ cup butter	75 mL
1 cup granulated sugar	250 mL
1 tsp vanilla	5 mL
½ tsp grated lemon peel	2 mL
4 eggs	4
3¾ cups all-purpose flour	925 mL
4 tsp baking powder	20 mL
¾ tsp freshly grated nutmeg	4 mL
½ tsp salt	2 mL
½ cup light cream	125 mL
Oil for frying	
½ cup (approx) icing sugar	125 mL

Croquignoles are crisp, twisted doughtnuts spiced with nutmeg and rich in eggs and butter. Although it's customary to serve them at Réveillon on Christmas Eve, they're good anytime, especially with mugs of hot chocolate after skiing or skating.

In a large bowl, cream together butter, granulated sugar, vanilla and lemon peel. Beat in the eggs, one at a time.

Mix together flour, baking powder, nutmeg and salt. Stir dry ingredients into the batter in 3 parts, alternating with the cream in 2 parts. The dough will be quite soft, but this results in more tender doughnuts. Cover and refrigerate for 2 to 3 hours or until firm.

Divide the dough into 4 parts. Work with 1 part at a time, refrigerating the remaining portions to keep them firm. On a well floured surface, roll out one portion of dough about ¼-inch (5 mm) thick. Cut strips of dough ¾-inch (2 cm) wide and 6 inches (15 cm) long. Twist each strip 3 times, then join ends by dampening with a drop of water and pinching together firmly.

Heat about 3 inches (7 cm) of oil to 360°F (185°C). Fry the croquignoles until golden, 1 to 1½ minutes per side. Remove with a slotted spoon and drain on paper towels. Repeat the rolling, shaping and frying with the rest of the dough, always keeping any unused dough in the refrigerator to keep it firm.

Place the doughnuts on a large serving platter or tray and sprinkle icing sugar generously over the tops. Serve as fresh as possible.

Makes about 48 croquignoles.

Deep Orange Squash and Spice Loaf

1¾ cups all-purpose flour	425 mL
1 tsp soda	5 mL
1 tsp cinnamon	5 mL
½ tsp baking powder	2 mL
½ tsp salt	2 mL
½ tsp freshly grated nutmeg	2 mL
½ tsp ginger	2 mL
¼ tsp allspice	1 mL
½ cup chopped, freshly shelled walnuts, pecans or hazelnuts	125 mL
½ cup currants	125 mL
3 eggs	3
½ cup butter, melted	125 mL
¼ cup buttermilk	50 mL
⅔ cup firmly packed brown sugar	150 mL
1½ cups mashed cooked squash	375 mL
1 tbsp grated orange peel	15 mL

The next time you prepare squash as a vegetable, cook extra for this moist, spicy, amber orange loaf. Slice and serve plain or with butter.

Grease a 9 x 5-inch (2 L) loaf pan and line the bottom with waxed paper. Grease the paper lightly and set aside.

Sift together flour, soda, cinnamon, baking powder, salt, nutmeg, ginger and allspice into a large bowl. Stir in the nuts and currants.

In a smaller bowl, beat together eggs, butter, buttermilk, sugar, squash and orange peel. Pour over the dry ingredients and mix just until blended.

Transfer batter to prepared pan and bake at 350°F (180°C) for 50 to 60 minutes or until a skewer inserted in the middle comes out clean. Let cool in the pan for 10 minutes, then turn out onto a rack and let cool, right side up. Wrap well and store in an airtight container for a day before slicing.

Makes 1 loaf.

Maple Syrup Buns

1 tsp granulated sugar	5 mL
½ cup lukewarm water	125 mL
1 pkg active dry yeast (1 tbsp/15 mL)	1
1 cup milk	250 mL
½ cup shortening	125 mL
¼ cup butter	50 mL
½ cup granulated sugar	125 mL

Looking for something patriotic and scrumptious to serve with back bacon? Look no further than these mouthwatering raisin-maple buns.

Dissolve 1 tsp (5 mL) sugar in the water. Sprinkle yeast over liquid and let stand for 10 minutes or until frothy.

Scald the milk and pour over the shortening, butter and sugar in a large bowl. Stir until the solids have melted, then

1 cup thoroughly mashed or riced mealy potatoes	250 mL
5½ cups (approx) all-purpose flour	1.375 L
2 eggs, beaten	2
1 tbsp cinnamon	15 mL
2 tsp salt	10 mL
1½ cups golden raisins	375 mL

GLAZE:

½ cup maple syrup	125 mL
1 tbsp granulated sugar	15 mL

add the potatoes, 1 cup (250 mL) of the flour, eggs, cinnamon and salt. Let cool to lukewarm and stir in the yeast mixture. Cover the bowl with a very damp tea towel. Let rise in a warm spot for 2 hours to form a sponge.

Cover the raisins with boiling water and let stand for 5 minutes. Drain, pat raisins dry with towelling and set aside.

Mix the remaining flour into the sponge about 1 cup (250 mL) at a time until dough is too stiff to stir. Sprinkle some of the flour onto the counter and transfer dough to counter. Knead in as much of the flour as necessary to form a silky firm dough. This usually takes 8 to 10 minutes, depending on the vigour of the baker. Mixing may be done throughout by machine.

Roll out dough to 1-inch (2.5 cm) thickness. Scatter the raisins over the surface of the dough and roll up jelly roll fashion. Fold in thirds and place in a greased bowl. Turn to grease on all sides. Cover the dough with greased waxed paper and the bowl with a very damp tea towel. Let rise in a warm place until doubled in bulk, 1½ to 2 hours.

Punch down dough, kneading briefly to distribute the raisins. Divide the dough in two; form each portion into a long sausage and cut each sausage into 12 pieces. Shape each piece into a round bun. Place buns in two greased 13 x 9-inch (4 L) pans, 12 buns to a pan. Cover each pan with greased waxed paper and a damp towel and let rise in a warm place until doubled in bulk, about 1½ hours.

Bake at 375° F (190° C) for 20 minutes or until browned. When the buns are almost done, combine the syrup and the sugar in a small saucepan for the glaze. Bring to a boil and boil for 3 minutes. Remove the buns from the pans and set upright on racks. Immediately brush or drizzle the glaze over the top and let cool.

Makes 24 buns.

Whole Wheat Buttermilk Rolls

1 tbsp granulated sugar	15 mL
½ cup lukewarm water	125 mL
2 pkg active dry yeast (2 tbsp/25 mL)	2
2 cups buttermilk	500 mL
2 cups water	500 mL
1 tbsp lard	15 mL
3 tbsp granulated sugar	50 mL
4 cups all-purpose flour, preferably unbleached	1 L
5 cups (approx) whole wheat flour	1.25 L

These delicious whole wheat rolls come from the kitchens of Gibson House, a restored 1850s gentleman's farmhouse in North York, Ontario.

Serve rolls stuffed with cold meat or cheese for a picnic.

Dissolve 1 tbsp (15 mL) sugar in the lukewarm water. Sprinkle yeast over liquid and let stand for 10 minutes or until frothy.

Meanwhile, heat the buttermilk and water together until steaming. Don't be alarmed if the buttermilk curdles; just stir it. Pour into a large mixing bowl. Add the lard and sugar, stirring until dissolved. Let cool to lukewarm. Using a fork, stir the yeast mixture to ensure all granules are dissolved and stir into the milk mixture.

Beat in the all-purpose flour and as much of the whole wheat flour as possible. Turn dough out onto a lightly floured counter and knead, incorporating as much of the remaining whole wheat flour as necessary to make a dough that isn't sticky (you may need up to 1 cup/250 mL more whole wheat flour). Continue kneading until dough is smooth and elastic, 8 to 10 minutes depending on the vigour of your kneading. Mixing may be done throughout by machine.

Place dough in a greased bowl, turning dough to grease all sides. Cover dough with greased waxed paper and bowl with a damp tea towel. Let rise until doubled in bulk, about 1 hour.

Punch down dough, knead briefly and let rest for 5 minutes for easy handling. Form dough into a long sausage and, using a sharp knife, cut into 24 equal pieces. Tuck ends under to form smooth rolls and place 2 inches (5 cm) apart on greased baking sheets. Cover with greased waxed paper and a damp tea towel and let rise until doubled in bulk, about 1 hour.

Bake at 375°F (190°C) for 35 to 40 minutes. Let cool on a rack.

Makes 24 rolls.

Onion Rolls

1 cup milk	250 mL
1 tsp salt	5 mL
2 tbsp butter	25 mL
1 tsp granulated sugar	5 mL
¼ cup lukewarm water	50 mL
1 pkg active dry yeast (1 tbsp/15 mL)	1
1 egg	1
3½ cups (approx) unbleached all-purpose flour	875 mL

FILLING:

3 tbsp butter	50 mL
3 cups very finely chopped onions	750 mL
1 tsp chopped fresh sage or ½ tsp (2 mL) crumbled dried	5 mL
Salt and freshly ground pepper	
1½ cups freshly grated Parmesan cheese (3 oz/100 g)	375 mL

GLAZE:

1 egg yolk	1
1 tbsp water	15 mL
¼ cup sesame seeds	50 mL

Unlike round onion buns, which have onion on top, these rolls are layered with finely chopped onions sautéed in butter with a touch of sage. Good with eggs for breakfast or brunch, and with salads and cold meats.

Heat milk, salt and butter just until butter is melted. Let cool to lukewarm.

In a large bowl, stir together sugar and water. Sprinkle yeast over liquid and let stand for 10 minutes or until frothy. Stir vigorously with a fork.

Pour butter mixture over yeast. Add egg and beat well. Begin adding flour, 1 cup (250 mL) at a time, until dough is too stiff to stir. Generously sprinkle some of the remaining flour on the counter and knead dough vigourously until smooth and silky, adding more flour if needed. Mixing may be done throughout by machine.

Place dough in a large greased bowl; turn dough to grease all sides. Cover the dough with greased waxed paper and bowl with a damp tea towel. Let rise in a warm spot until doubled in bulk, about 1 hour.

FILLING: In a skillet over low heat, melt butter and fry onions very gently until golden, 30 to 40 minutes, stirring occasionally. Season with sage, salt and pepper and let cool.

Punch down dough and divide in half. On a lightly floured counter, roll out each portion into a rectangle about 12 x 8 inches (30 x 20 cm). Spread half the onions and cheese over the dough, leaving a ½-inch (1 cm) border along the long side at the top. Roll from bottom to top, jelly roll fashion, and pinch seam together. Cut into 8 slices. Repeat with remaining dough and onions. Transfer to greased baking sheets. Cover lightly with greased waxed paper and a damp tea towel, and let rise until doubled in bulk, 45 to 60 minutes.

Stir together egg yolk and water and brush lightly over rolls. Sprinkle with sesame seeds. Bake at 350°F (180°C) for about 30 minutes or until nicely browned and rolls sound hollow when tapped. Let cool on racks.

Makes 16 large rolls.

Cheddar Cheese Bread

1 pkg active dry yeast (1 tbsp/15 mL)	1
1/4 cup lukewarm water	50 mL
1 3/4 cups milk	425 mL
1/4 cup granulated sugar	50 mL
2 tsp salt	10 mL
2 tbsp butter	25 mL
3 cups grated old Cheddar cheese (12 oz/375 g)	750 mL
5 1/2 cups (approx) all-purpose flour	1.375 L
1 egg yolk	1
2 tbsp light cream or milk	25 mL
1/4 cup sesame seeds	50 mL

Last spring I had the chance to watch Rose Murray teaching the art of bread-making at Conestoga College in Waterloo, Ontario. Her recipe for Cheddar cheese bread appealed to the students' appetites and caught my fancy as well. It's different from many cheese breads. Instead of being full of cheese chunks, Rose's bread has the mellow flavour of Cheddar throughout, and a crunchy sprinkle of sesame seeds on top. Great with cold meats and salads; superb toasted.

In a small bowl, sprinkle yeast over water and let stand for 10 minutes or until frothy.

In a medium saucepan, heat milk to scalding (small bubbles form around edges of pan). Stir in sugar, salt, butter and 2 cups (500 mL) of the cheese. Stir until butter and cheese have melted, then set aside to cool to lukewarm (it may be handy to refrigerate the mixture).

In a large mixing bowl, combine 2 1/2 cups (625 mL) of the flour, the milk mixture, the yeast and remaining cheese. Beat by hand or with a mixer until batter is smooth and very elastic.

Add the remaining flour about 1/2 cup (125 mL) at a time, stirring by hand or with the mixer. When dough starts to leave the sides of the bowl, either turn out onto a floured counter and knead until dough is smooth and springy, about 10 minutes or change to dough hook, kneading for about 7 minutes.

Place dough in greased bowl; turn to grease on all sides. Cover dough with greased waxed paper and bowl with a damp tea towel. Let rise in a warm spot until doubled in bulk, about 1 hour.

Punch down dough and turn out onto floured counter. Divide in half. Cover lightly and let rest for 10 minutes for easier shaping. Divide each half into 3 parts and roll each part into ropes, about 12 to 14 inches (30 to 35 cm) long and braid together.

Grease two 9 x 5-inch (2 L) bread or loaf pans well and carefully place loaves in them. Cover with greased waxed paper and return them to a warm place. Cover lightly with a damp tea towel. Let rise until doubled in bulk, 45 to 60 minutes.

Mix together the egg yolk and cream and brush very gently over surface of bread. Sprinkle with sesame seeds. Bake at 375°F (190°C) for 40 minutes or until the loaves sound hollow when lightly tapped. The loaves brown quickly because of the egg wash; watch carefully after 15 minutes and cover lightly with foil if necessary to prevent over-browning.

Remove bread from pans as soon as they are done and set on racks to cool.

Makes 2 loaves.

Kosuniak

1 cup milk	250 mL
1 cup granulated sugar	250 mL
2 tsp grated lemon peel	10 mL
2 tsp granulated sugar	10 mL
¾ cup lukewarm water	175 mL
2 pkg active dry yeast (2 tbsp/25 mL)	2
⅓ cup butter	75 mL
3 eggs	3
6 cups (approx) all-purpose flour	1.5 L

TOPPING:

1 egg	1
2 tbsp sesame seeds	25 mL

The recipe for this traditional Macedonian Easter bread is adapted from a very detailed one in *Traditional Macedonian Recipes*. This collection of heritage recipes was first printed in 1969 by the Ladies' Auxiliary of St. George's Macedono-Bulgarian Eastern Orthodox Church on Regent Street, in what was once the heart of Toronto's Macedonian community. The bread is light, almost cake-like, and baked with a sprinkle of sesame seeds. It is a tradition to make many loaves of kosuniak and offer them to family and friends.

In a small saucepan, warm milk, 1 cup (250 mL) sugar and lemon peel just until sugar is dissolved.

Dissolve 2 tsp (10 mL) sugar in lukewarm water. Sprinkle yeast over liquid and let stand for 10 minutes or until frothy.

Melt butter and let cool. Beat eggs; combine with butter, and milk and yeast mixtures.

Scoop 5 cups (1.25 L) of the flour into a large bowl. Make a well in the centre. Pour in half the liquid and, using one hand, mix in flour from the sides of the bowl. Blend in remaining milk mixture, continuing to use your hand. Still working in the bowl, knead in about another ½ cup (125 mL) of the flour. Note the dough is still very soft at this stage. Mixing may be done throughout by machine.

Sprinkle counter generously with a few tablespoons of flour. Transfer dough to counter and knead, incorporating enough flour to make a satiny smooth dough, 10 to 15 minutes. Form into a smooth ball.

Place dough in a large greased bowl, turning dough to grease on all sides. Cover dough with greased wax paper and bowl with damp tea towel. Let rise in a warm spot until doubled in bulk, about 1½ hours.

Butter two 9 x 5-inch (2 L) loaf pans and an area of the counter about 12 inches (30 cm) square. Punch down dough; roll out on buttered counter into a rectangle about 12 inches (30 cm) wide and 9 inches (23 cm) long. Cut into 6 strips, each 2 inches (5 cm) wide and 9 inches (23 cm) long. Twirl 3 strips slightly and braid. Tuck ends under firmly and place in pan. Repeat with remaining 3 strips. Brush tops lightly with butter.

Cover loaves lightly with greased waxed paper and a damp towel. Let rise in a warm spot until doubled in bulk, about 1¼ hours.

TOPPING: Beat egg lightly and brush over tops of loaves. Sprinkle with sesame seeds.

Bake at 350°F (180°C) for 40 minutes or until golden brown and loaves sound hollow when lightly tapped. Remove from pans and let cool on racks.

Makes 2 large loaves.

Pane Dulce di Pasqua — Cazuppa

1 cup water	250 mL	
1 cup milk	250 mL	
$1\frac{1}{2}$ cups granulated sugar	375 mL	
1 tsp salt	5 mL	
1 tbsp grated lemon peel	15 mL	
$\frac{1}{4}$ cup lemon juice	50 mL	
1 cup oil	250 mL	
$\frac{1}{2}$ cup lukewarm water	125 mL	
1 tbsp granulated sugar	15 mL	
2 pkg active dry yeast (2 tbsp/25 mL)	2	
6 eggs	6	
10 cups (approx) all-purpose flour	2.5 L	

TOPPING:

13 eggs	13
Easter egg dye in colours of your choice (not purple — it's for Advent)	

At Villa Colombo, the Italian community's home for the aged in Metro Toronto, residents begin Easter morning with coffee and cazuppa, a special braided sweet bread made festive with red, blue, green and yellow eggs baked right in the tresses. According to Ramona Cameletti, dietitian and food services manager at the Villa, there are many different Italian Easter breads or *pane dulce di Pasqua*. The one baked at the Villa has its origins in the southern province of Calabria.

Jackie Rosati of the Villa Colombo Ladies' Auxiliary makes cazuppa at Easter and her recipe, halved, is as follows.

Bring 1 cup (250 mL) water, milk, $1\frac{1}{2}$ cups (375 mL) sugar and salt to the scalding point (bubbles form around edges of pan). Let cool and stir in lemon peel, juice and oil.

Combine lukewarm water and 1 tbsp (15 mL) sugar. Sprinkle yeast over liquid and let stand for 10 minutes or until frothy. Beat eggs in a large bowl, using an electric mixer if possible. Stir first the milk mixture, then the yeast mixture into the eggs.

Continuing to beat, begin adding the flour. When batter becomes too thick to manage with beaters, either change to a dough hook and knead in enough of the remaining flour to make a silky dough or mix by hand, adding flour until dough is firm enough to transfer to a well floured counter. Continue kneading on the counter for about 15 minutes, adding as much of the flour as is necessary to make a smooth dough that is not sticky.

Shape dough into a smooth ball and place in a large greased bowl, turning dough to grease all sides. Cover dough with greased wax paper and bowl with a damp tea towel. Let rise until doubled in bulk, about $1\frac{1}{2}$ hours. Punch down and let rest for 20 minutes to relax dough.

Meanwhile, dye 12 eggs for the topping in a variety of colours and let dry. Do not hard-cook the eggs before dying; they cook as the bread bakes. Beat remaining egg and set aside. Grease 2 large baking sheets.

Divide the dough into 8 equal parts. Roll into ropes about 24 inches (60 cm) long. Twist 4 ropes and braid. Form into a circle (this makes the braided nest) and transfer to baking sheet. Repeat with remaining 4 ropes. Nestle eggs into the folds of the braids. Cover lightly with greased waxed paper and a damp towel and let rise until doubled in bulk, about 1 hour. Brush surface of braids with beaten egg.

Bake at 350°F (180°C) for about 30 minutes or until rich golden brown and loaves sound hollow when gently tapped. Transfer to racks to cool.

Serve very fresh, offering the now hard-cooked eggs along with the bread.

Makes 2 large braids.

Barmbrack

1 tsp granulated sugar	5 mL
⅓ cup lukewarm water	75 mL
1 pkg active dry yeast (1 tbsp/15 mL)	1
⅔ cup granulated sugar	150 mL
1 tsp salt	5 mL
1 tsp allspice	5 mL
½ cup butter, softened	125 mL
1 cup milk	250 mL
1 cup currants	250 mL
½ cup raisins	125 mL
½ cup mixed candied peel	125 mL
5 cups (approx) all-purpose flour	1.25 L
3 eggs, beaten	3

GLAZE:

2 tsp butter, melted	10 mL
2 tsp granulated sugar	10 mL

Barmbrack is a "freckled" spicy yeast bread of Irish origin. The "freckles" are currants, along with raisins and mixed fruit in this version.

Dissolve 1 tsp (5 mL) sugar in the water. Sprinkle yeast over liquid and let stand for 10 minutes or until frothy.

Combine ⅔ cup (150 mL) sugar, salt, allspice, butter and milk in a saucepan. Heat, stirring frequently, just until the sugar is dissolved and the butter is melted. Let cool to lukewarm.

Toss the currants, raisins and peel with about 2 tbsp (25 mL) of the flour and set aside.

Stir the yeast mixture with a fork and blend together with the eggs and cooled milk mixture in a large bowl. Using a wooden spoon or a mixer, beat in the flour, about 1 cup (250 mL) at a time, until the dough is too firm to mix. Knead in the remaining flour, either in the bowl or on the counter, sprinkling with a little more flour if necessary to make a satiny smooth dough. Mixing may be done up to this point by machine. Knead in the fruit and place in a large greased bowl; turn dough to grease all sides. Cover the dough with greased waxed paper and bowl with a damp tea towel. Let rise in a warm place until doubled in bulk, about 1½ hours.

Punch down dough. Form into 2 loaves and place in two buttered 9 x 5-inch (2 L) loaf pans. Cover the surface of the loaves with greased waxed paper and the pans with a damp tea towel. Let rise in a warm place until doubled in bulk, about 1½ hours. Bake at 350°F (180°C) for 30 minutes or until the loaves sound hollow when lightly tapped.

Remove from the pans and set on racks. Brush the tops with melted butter and sprinkle with remaining sugar. Let cool thoroughly and slice.

Makes 2 medium loaves.

DRINKS

Our taste in drinks is changing. Canadians are shifting away from spirits to lighter, less alcoholic and lower-calorie beverages. Nowhere is this shift more obvious than in our attitude to wine. Ten years ago, when I wrote *Classic Canadian Cooking*, the Canadian wine industry was just beginning to respond to the desire for quality Canadian wines to accompany food. The years since have seen the industry flourish and mature, exceeding many wine lovers' wildest dreams. Ontario and British Columbia are producing fine wines from grapes grown in fields that used to yield peaches and wheat.

There are many occasions when non-alcoholic but special drinks are in order. When entertaining, it's considerate to offer a frosty iced tea or coffee, a big bowl of carefully blended fruit punch or simply a selection of sparkling waters and juices, along with the spirits and wine. The following recipes should offer some refreshing possibilities to suit all occasions.

Iced Mint Tea

A special iced tea with the fragrance and taste of mint. Enjoy it in the summer when the mint is fresh.

1 cup packed fresh mint leaves	250 mL
2 tbsp loose tea (2 tea bags), Earl Grey recommended	25 mL
½ cup granulated sugar	125 mL
2 strips lemon peel	2
4 cups boiling water	1 L
⅓ cup lemon juice	75 mL
Ice cubes	
4 lemon slices	4
4 mint sprigs	4

Combine mint, tea, sugar and lemon peel in a medium bowl and cover with the boiling water. Let steep for 15 minutes; strain. Let cool completely and blend in lemon juice.

To serve, half-fill 4 glasses with ice cubes. Pour in mint tea and garnish each glass with a lemon slice and mint sprig.

Makes 4 or 5 drinks.

Frosty Viennese Coffee with Chocolate

Ice cubes	
3 cups cold, strong, continental roast coffee	750 mL
⅔ cup light cream or milk	150 mL
1 tbsp Sugar Syrup (see below)	15 mL
½ cup whipping cream	125 mL
1 tbsp semisweet chocolate shavings or generous shake of cocoa	15 mL

A welcome cold coffee break. Freshly ground coffee always makes the best cup or, in this case, glass.

Distribute ice cubes among 3 tall glasses. Pour in cold coffee, light cream and sugar syrup. Stir well. Whip remaining cream and top each glass with a generous dollop and a sprinkle of chocolate shavings.

Makes 3 frosty glasses.

Sugar Syrup

2 cups granulated sugar	500 mL
2 cups water	500 mL

Keep a jar of this in the refrigerator and use to sweeten iced tea, coffee and lemonade. A small spoonful in each glass is usually enough.

Combine sugar and water in a saucepan and bring to a boil. Boil for 2 minutes. Pour into a clean jar and store in the refrigerator.

Makes about 3 cups (750 mL) syrup.

Watermelon Slush

6 cups chopped, seeded watermelon, in 1-inch (2.5 cm) cubes	1.5 L
½ cup instant dissolving sugar	125 mL
¼ tsp grated lemon or orange peel	1 mL
2 tbsp lemon or orange juice	25 mL
Mint sprigs	

Better than cold watermelon slices on a hot day. Serve this rosy pink slush in glasses and eat it with a spoon. Or serve in individual paper cones and slurp them outdoors.

Place watermelon, sugar, peel and juice in a food processor or blender and process until smooth. Transfer to a 13 x 9-inch (4 L) cake pan and freeze until solid around the edges but still mushy in the middle. This usually takes 1 to 1½ hours but the time can vary.

Transfer the semi-frozen watermelon to a food processor or blender and process until smooth. Spoon immediately into chilled glasses and garnish with mint. (If there is a delay in serving, return purée to the pan and refreeze. At serving time, let it soften slightly in the refrigerator for 15 minutes. Blend or process again before serving.)

Makes 6 servings.

Lassi

½ cup natural yogurt	125 mL
½ cup cold water	125 mL
1 tsp granulated sugar	5 mL
¼ tsp cardamom	1 mL
¼ tsp rose water	1 mL
Ice cubes	
1 tsp chopped natural pistachios (unsalted and undyed)	5 mL

This yogurt-based Indian drink is the ultimate tangy refreshment. Serve it on its own or with spicy food. Rose water is available in Indian, Jamaican, Middle Eastern and specialty food shops or in drugstores.

Combine yogurt, water, sugar, cardamom and rose water. Pour into a tall, ice-filled glass. Sprinkle with pistachios and serve immediately.

Makes 1 serving.

Big Party Punch

3 cans (each 48 oz/1.3 L) unsweetened pineapple juice		3
3 cups orange juice		750 mL
1½ cups lemon juice		375 mL
⅓ cup lime juice		75 mL
2 cups granulated sugar (optional)		500 mL
1 cup loosely packed fresh mint leaves		250 mL
Ice block or ring frozen in tube pan		
2 bottles (each 750 mL) ginger ale		2
1 bottle (750 mL) soda water		1
2 cups strawberries, hulled and halved		500 mL
2 each oranges, lemons and limes		2

Everybody seems to want a good punch recipe and you should keep this one from Gail Schioler's *The Non-Drinker's Drink Book* in mind for your next reception or open house. The mint and lime give the punch a little nip and I suggest bruising the mint in the juice before chilling. Of course, you can vary the fruit garnish according to the season — citrus in the winter, berries in the spring and summer.

Combine juices, sugar, if using, and mint leaves in a punch bowl. Chill for at least 2 hours. Strain or remove leaves. Place ice in the bowl. Carefully pour ginger ale and soda water down the side of the bowl. Add strawberries. Slice citrus fruit and float on top.

Makes about 80 punch cup-size servings.

Raspberry Champagne

1 ice cube		1
1 raspberry		1
½ cup concentrated raspberry juice		125 mL
½ cup (approx) chilled dry champagne or sparkling wine		125 mL

Concentrated raspberry juice from British Columbia makes a most refreshing non-alcoholic drink, or marries with champagne for special occasions. Look for it in the frozen food section of your supermarket.

Place ice and raspberry in a stemmed wine glass. Pour in raspberry juice and top with champagne. Stir gently just to combine.

Makes 1 drink, worth doubling.

May Wine Bowl

12 sprigs woodruff, each about 3 inches (8 cm) long	12
¼ cup granulated sugar	50 mL
¼ cup brandy	50 mL
1 strip orange peel	1
2 bottles (each 750 mL) Rhine wine or other fruity but dry white wine	2
Ice	
1 bottle (750 mL) sparkling white wine or soda water, chilled	1
2 cups small strawberries, hulled and halved	500 mL

A perfect punch for spring weddings or, for that matter, parties or receptions of any kind. Woodruff plants are available at good herb greenhouses.

Combine woodruff, sugar, brandy, orange peel and 1 bottle of Rhine wine. Cover and let stand for 1 to 2 hours at room temperature, bruising the woodruff occasionally with a wooden spoon.

Remove and discard the woodruff and orange peel. Place the ice in a large bowl; pour in the woodruff-scented wine, remaining Rhine wine and sparkling wine. Stir gently. Float the strawberries on top. Serve while still fizzy and include a berry in each glass.

Makes 18 servings, ½ cup (125 mL) each.

Maud Fuller's Sorrel "Refresher"

2 oz dried sorrel	60 g
⅓ cup grated fresh ginger	75 mL
2 strips orange peel	2
Pinch freshly grated nutmeg	Pinch
8 cups boiling water	2 L
⅔ cup firmly packed dark brown sugar	150 mL
2 tbsp fresh lime juice	25 mL
3 cups port	750 mL
½ cup white rum	125 mL

Look for dried sorrel in Latin American and West Indian stores and choose packages with whole blossoms inside. The combination of ruby-red sorrel, fresh ginger, port and rum makes a very refreshing summer drink when served in tall glasses with ice. Do as Maud Fuller does — steep, strain and store the sorrel in the refrigerator for up to several weeks and have it ready to offer guests.

In a heatproof pitcher or bowl, combine sorrel, ginger, orange peel, nutmeg and water. Stir, let cool and cover lightly. Let stand for 1 day at room temperature.

Strain into a large bowl and blend in the remaining ingredients. Transfer to large clean bottles or canning jars and store in the refrigerator. To serve, pour into ice-filled glasses.

Makes 12 to 15 servings.

Cocoa

2 cups granulated sugar	500 mL
1 cup cocoa	250 mL
½ tsp cinnamon	2 mL
¼ tsp salt	1 mL
2 cups boiling water	500 mL
2 tsp vanilla	10 mL
Milk	

This recipe came to light in *Kitchen Lore,* recipes compiled about 60 years ago by the Ladies' Aid Society of St. Paul's Eastern United Church in Ottawa. Cups of cocoa (never "hot chocolate" in the Ottawa Valley) were a grand way to welcome skaters home after a night at one of the Valley's outdoor skating rinks.

In a medium saucepan, blend together sugar, cocoa, cinnamon and salt. Whisking constantly, pour in the boiling water. Place over high heat and bring to a boil. Reduce heat and simmer gently, uncovered, for 10 minutes, stirring frequently. Let cool, stir in vanilla and pour into a clean jar.

Makes about 3 cups (750 mL) syrup. To enjoy, stir 1 to 2 tbsp (15 to 25 mL) into a glass of cold milk, or heat syrup and milk together until steaming. Serve with a splash of brandy or coffee liqueur or with dollops of whipped cream.

PRESERVES

After a few decades on the back burner, preserving is once more considered an important part of cooking. It's become rather chic, in fact, to put down your own jams, jellies, chutneys, relishes and pickles. Preservers have found that the fruit of their labours make great gifts.

It's doubtful that urban Canadians — which is what more and more of us are — will ever feel the need to preserve whole shelves full of fruit and vegetables for winter eating. And for people who still want to preserve their harvest, freezing has put an end to hot summer days over the canner. Nevertheless, many busy homemakers, weekend perservers and after-work cooks can still take pride in making some of the household's favourite sweets and sours when they have the time.

Preparing Jars

For jams, jellies and marmalades, reusable jars make economical receptacles. For relishes, pickles and sour sauces, buy preserving jars with two-piece lids. Every time the jar is filled, you will need to replace the disk, but the screw band can be reused as long as it is not rusty or bent. Choose sizes that suit your household needs. Jars are available in 8-, 16- and 32-oz (250 mL, 500 mL and 1 L) sizes.

The preparation of the jars is the same for all preserves. Check that there are no nicks or cracks. Wash the jars in warm soapy water and rinse. Place on a metal tray or jelly roll pan. Include on the tray a set of tongs, a metal funnel and measuring cup (the ½ cup/125 mL size is the one I find most convenient). For chunky preserves, include an all-metal table knife.

Time the sterilization period to co-incide with the time your preserve should be ready for bottling. The jars must be heated for 15 minutes at 225°F (110°C) and if they are ready a few minutes before the preserve, just leave them in the hot oven with the heat turned off. Use the tongs to take them out as you fill them.

Place the disks in a small saucepan. Cover with boiling water and boil for 5 minutes, again co-ordinating the timing with the end of the preserving. Leave disks in the hot water until needed if you are a few minutes longer than you expected.

A pair of oven mitts is obviously a preserver's best friend.

Setting Point

There are several ways to tell if jelly, jam or marmalade is set. You can test the preserves with a candy thermometer. When the thermometer registers 218°F (104°C), the setting point has been reached.

To test jam or marmalade without a thermometer: Place two plates in the freezer before starting. After about 4 minutes of boiling, begin testing by dropping a small spoonful of preserve on one of the plates. Let cool, then run your finger through the preserve. If the surface wrinkles, the setting point has been reached.

To test jelly without a thermometer: Dip a large spoon into the pan. Hold the spoon horizontally above the steam. At first, the liquid runs off quickly in two streams. As the jelling-stage approaches, the two streams slow down and finally, two drops merge and hang from the spoon as one.

Filling Jars

For jams and other sweet thick preserves, insert funnel into jar. Scoop jam into the funnel, lifting the funnel as the jar fills. Leave a ½-inch (1 cm) headspace at the top of the jar and be careful not to smear the inside of the jar above the top level of jam. Let it cool for 10 minutes.

For relishes and pickles, fill preserving jars in same manner, but leave ¼-inch (5 mm) headspace. Use knife to press out any air bubbles if preserve has large pieces of vegetables. Re-establish headspace if necessary. Take care not to smear relish on the top rim of the jar. Wipe off any smears with a paper towel moistened in boiling water. Immediately cover with lids and screw on bands firmly.

Sealing Jam, Jelly and Marmalade Jars

Melt paraffin wax in a metal teapot or tall coffee can pinched at the top on one side to form a spout. *Never place paraffin wax over direct heat;* set the teapot or can in a shallow saucepan of water and heat over medium-low setting.

Pour a thin layer of melted paraffin over sweet preserve

that has cooled for 10 minutes. Tilt and rotate the jar to extend the wax seal to the top rim. Prick any air bubbles. Let wax harden and the preserve cool completely before applying a second thin layer of wax in the same manner. Let cool and cover with clean lids.

Storing Preserves
Wipe the jars, label and store away from heat, light and dampness. The old-fashioned fruit cellar with shelving along the outside wall is ideal; apartment dwellers and hot house dwellers will just have to find the best available place. Carefully made and sealed preserves should last for one year under proper storage conditions.

Whole Berry Strawberry Preserve

16 cups whole hulled strawberries	4 L
2 lemons	2
Granulated sugar	
2 to 4 tbsp cassis or kirsch	25 to 50 mL

Credit for the idea of simmering the berries before adding the sugar goes to Charlotte Sykes. She in turn learned it in Newfoundland, where homemade berry jam is a long-standing cooking tradition.

Prepare seven 8-ounce (250 mL) jars (see page 127). Set 2 plates in the freezer.

Place berries in a colander and rinse quickly but thoroughly in cold water. Drain and hull. Place about ¼ of the berries in a jam pan or large heavy saucepan and crush. Add remaining whole berries.

Squeeze lemons. Strain juice and pour into pan. Tie peels and any seeds in tightly woven cheesecloth. Toss in the pan and stir. Bring slowly to a boil; reduce heat and simmer, uncovered, for 1 hour. Squeeze lemon bag and discard.

Measure fruit and add an equal volume of sugar to the jam pan. Bring to a boil and boil hard, stirring frequently, until set, 10 to 12 minutes.

Skim off scum and stir for 3 to 5 minutes to keep fruit floating in the jelly. Stir in cassis and pour into prepared jars, leaving ½-inch (1 cm) headspace. Let cool for 10 minutes. Seal with wax (see page 128). Wipe jars, cover with clean lids and label. Store in cool, dark, dry place.

Makes about six 8-ounce (250 mL) jars.

Seedless Raspberry Preserve

10 cups raspberries (2 lb/1 kg)	2.5 L
¼ cup water	50 mL
4 cups (approx) granulated sugar	1 L
2 tbsp raspberry eau-de-vie (framboise), optional	25 mL

The price of raspberries has made them the berry of home gardeners, the well-to-do and those who pick their own. Reflecting this fruit's status, here is a preserve that further enhances the glorious raspberry flavour.

Prepare eleven 4-ounce (125 mL) jars (see page 127).

Place berries in a medium saucepan and crush. Cook, uncovered, at a bare simmer over medium-low heat for 10 to 15 minutes, crushing berries periodically to release all their juices.

Drain berries in a large sieve placed over a bowl and thoroughly press out all juice and pulp. Return seeds to the saucepan, add water and heat through. Pour back into the sieve and press again. This second pressing cleans most of the raspberry flavour off the seeds and now, in good conscience, you can throw the seeds away.

Measure the juice and pulp and pour into a jam pan or heavy saucepan with an equal volume of sugar. Mix well and bring to a boil over high heat. Stirring constantly, boil vigorously until the preserve sets, 5 to 8 minutes.

Remove from heat and skim off scum. Stir in framboise, if using, and pour into jars, leaving ½-inch (1 cm) headspace. Let cool for 10 minutes. Seal with wax (see page 128). Wipe jars, cover with clean lids and label. Store in a cool, dark, dry place.

Makes about ten 4-ounce (125 mL) jars.

Very Berry Jam

2 cups black currants	500 mL
1 cup water	250 mL
2 cups gooseberries, topped and tailed	500 mL
2 cups stemmed red currants	500 mL
2 cups raspberries	500 mL
2 cups sliced strawberries	500 mL
6 cups granulated sugar	1.5 L

A jam to remind you all winter long of the best fruits of summer. If you can't face a hot kitchen in July, freeze each fruit separately and fill the kitchen with berry patch perfumes on a cool fall day.

In a medium saucepan, bring the black currants and water to a boil. Cover, reduce heat and simmer for 10 minutes or until soft. Purée in a sieve or food mill and place purée in a jam pan or large heavy saucepan.

Add all the remaining fruit and stir together. Cover and bring to a simmer over medium heat, stirring frequently. Simmer for 10 minutes, stirring periodically.

Meanwhile, prepare eight 8-ounce (250 mL) jars (see page 127).

Stir in sugar, increase heat to high and boil until set, about 10 minutes, stirring constantly.

Remove from heat and skim off scum. Stir for 5 minutes, then ladle into jars, leaving ½-inch (1 cm) headspace. Let cool for 10 minutes. Seal with wax (see page 128). Wipe jars, cover with clean lids and label. Store in a cool, dark, dry place.

Makes about seven 8-ounce (250 mL) jars.

Classic Seville Orange Marmalade

2 lb Seville oranges	1 kg
Cold water	
Granulated sugar	

This is without a doubt the finest orange marmalade. Hats off to Helen Gougeon whose food writing encouraged me to start making marmalade.

Halve oranges; squeeze out juice and strain, reserving all seeds and loose membranes. Slice orange peel into thick or thin strips (up to ¼ inch/5 mm) according to your preference. Combine with the juice and measure into a large saucepan. There should be about 6 cups (1.5 L). Tie seeds and membranes loosely in a double thickness of tightly woven cheesecloth and add to the saucepan. Add water equal to the volume of peel and juice plus 1 cup (250 mL).

Bring to a boil; reduce heat to the barest simmer and cook, uncovered, until the peel is tender and translucent, about 2 hours. Periodically press the seeds to help extract the pectin. At the end of the simmering time, remove and discard seed bag after pressing out all thick slimy juices.

Prepare ten 8-ounce (250 mL) jars (see page 127).

Measure peel and liquid into a large heavy saucepan. Add an equal volume of sugar and, stirring constantly, bring to a boil over high heat. Boil hard until the marmalade sets, 20 to 25 minutes.

Skim off scum and pour marmalade into prepared jars, leaving ½-inch (1 cm) headspace. Let cool for 10 minutes. Seal with wax (see page 128). Wipe jars, cover with clean lids and label. Store in a cool, dark, dry place.

Makes about nine 8-ounce (250 mL) jars.

Brandied Apricot Tangerine Marmalade

1 lb dried apricots	500 g
8 cups water	2 L
6 large tangerines, mandarins or clementines	6
Granulated sugar	
½ cup slivered blanched almonds	125 mL
¼ cup apricot, mandarin or orange liqueur or brandy (optional)	50 mL

Here's a splendid winter preserve that's less work than other marmalades, but tastes as if you've laboured for hours. Serve on toast, biscuits, croissants or fresh rolls. Thin with orange juice, liqueur (apricot, mandarin or orange) or brandy and serve over cheesecakes, vanilla custards or fine ice creams.

Cut apricots into thin strips. Place in a large bowl, cover with half the water and set aside.

Slice tangerines very thinly and cut slices in half. Remove seeds and tie loosely in a double layer of tightly woven cheesecloth. Combine with the tangerine slices and remaining water in a saucepan. Cover and bring to a boil. Reduce heat to very low and simmer until the peel is tender, 20 to 30 minutes. Uncover and let cool. Add to apricots. Cover and let stand for 12 to 24 hours.

Prepare eleven 8-ounce (250 mL) jars (see page 127).

Measure the combined fruit; there should be about 10 cups (2.5 L). Transfer to a jam pan or large heavy saucepan and add ½ cup (125 mL) sugar for every 1 cup (250 mL) of fruit and juice. Mix well and bring to a boil. Boil hard, stirring very frequently, until the preserve thickens, 20 to 30 minutes. Stir in the almonds about 5 minutes before the end of the cooking time.

Remove from heat and skim off scum. Stir in liqueur if desired. Pour into jars, leaving ½-inch (1 cm) headspace. Let cool for 10 minutes. Seal with wax (see page 128). Wipe jars, cover with clean lids and label. Store in cool, dark, dry place.

Makes about ten 8-ounce (250 mL) jars.

Rhubarb and Orange Conserve

11 cups chopped pink rhubarb, in ½-inch (1 cm) pieces (2¾ lb/1.25 kg)	2.75 L
7 cups granulated sugar	1.75 L
2 oranges	2
8 thin slices lemon	8
1 cup water	250 mL
2 cups golden raisins	500 mL
1 cup coarsely chopped, freshly shelled walnuts	250 mL

The arrival of rhubarb in the spring is the best excuse I know to get out the preserving pan and make the season's first batch of jam. A conserve like this with lemon slices, golden raisins and crunchy walnuts can't be bought except in specialty shops at fancy prices.

In a large glass bowl, layer rhubarb and sugar; cover lightly and let stand overnight at room temperature.

Prepare ten 8-ounce (250 mL) jars (see page 127).

Slice oranges thinly. Combine with lemon slices and water in a small saucepan. Cover and cook over low heat for 20 to 30 minutes or until peel is tender and translucent.

In a jam pan or large heavy saucepan, stir together citrus fruit mixture, rhubarb with sugar and raisins. Bring to a boil, stirring constantly. Cook for about 20 minutes, stirring unflaggingly and adjusting the heat so the conserve bubbles briskly but doesn't scorch. Add walnuts and cook for 5 minutes longer or until conserve has thickened and set.

Remove from heat and skim off scum. Pour into jars, leaving ½-inch (1 cm) headspace. Let cool for 10 minutes. Seal with wax (see page 128). Wipe jars, cover with clean lids and store in cool, dark, dry place.

Makes about nine 8-ounce (250 mL) jars.

Niagara Peninsula Conserve

4 oranges	4
½ cup water	125 mL
cups sliced stoned peaches (4½ lb/2 kg)	2 L
ps quartered stoned ums (1½ lb/750 g)	1 L
s sliced stoned tarines (1½ lb/750 g)	1 L
ated sugar	
ultana raisins, n or dark	500 mL

This is a recipe to keep on hand as the different varieties of peaches and plums come onto the market in the summer and early fall. Early in the season, combine peaches with yellow plums and light sultanas for a gloriously orange conserve. Later, use red or purple prune plums and dark raisins for a conserve with rich ruby purple hues. Neither the plums nor the nectarines need to be peeled.

Quarter oranges lengthwise and cut 2 sections at a time crosswise into thin slices. Remove and discard any seeds. Place orange slices and water in a large saucepan. Cover and simmer over low heat, stirring periodically, for 20 to 30 minutes or until tender.

Add peaches, plums and nectarines. Bring to a gentle boil over medium heat and cook, uncovered, for 10 minutes, stirring frequently.

Prepare sixteen 8-ounce (250 mL) jars (see page 127).

Measure the fruit; there should be about 12 cups (3 L). Divide in half. In a jam pan or heavy saucepan, combine each portion with an equal volume of sugar. Stir in half the raisins and bring to a rapid boil over high heat. Boil until the conserve sets, 12 to 15 minutes, stirring almost constantly.

Remove from heat and skim off scum. Pour into jars, leaving ½-inch (1 cm) headspace. Let cool for 10 minutes. Seal with wax (see page 128). Wipe jars, cover with clean lids and label. Store in cool , dark, dry place.

Makes about fifteen 8-ounce (250 mL) jars.

Note: For a tarter conserve with a softer set, use ¾ cup (175 mL) sugar for every 1 cup (250 mL) of prepared fruit.

Grape Jelly with Fresh Basil

8 cups stemmed Concord grapes	2 L
2½ cups water	625 mL
½ cup packed chopped fresh basil leaves and stems	125 mL
Granulated sugar	

Concord grapes make a royal purple jelly. With the added flavour of basil, this jelly can do double duty — at the breakfast table and alongside duck, partridge or venison. Choose the grapes for this jelly early in the season, when half of them are slightly underripe and greenish.

Combine grapes, water and basil in a large saucepan and bring to a boil, mashing the fruit frequently. Reduce heat and simmer, uncovered, for 10 minutes or until grapes are soft.

Transfer mixture to a dampened jelly bag or colander lined with a double thickness of damp fine cheesecloth. Let drip for 4 hours or overnight.

Prepare five 8-ounce (250 mL) jars (see page 127).

Measure the juice; there should be about 4 cups (1 L). Combine juice with an equal volume of sugar in a jam pan or heavy saucepan and bring to a boil. Stirring frequently, boil hard for 12 to 14 minutes or until jelly stage is reached.

Remove from heat and skim off scum. Pour into jars, leaving ½-inch (1 cm) headspace. Let cool for 10 minutes. Seal with wax (see page 128). Wipe jars, cover with clean lids and label. Store in a cool, dark, dry place.

Makes about four 8-ounce (250 mL) jars.

Lemon Rosemary Jelly

8 large lemons	8
14 cups water	3.5 L
⅔ cup coarsely chopped fresh rosemary sprigs	150 mL
Granulated sugar	
12 sprigs fresh rosemary, about 3 inches (7 cm) long	12

A beautiful jelly, tart and lemony, yet scented with rosemary. With a sprig of rosemary set in the clear yellow jelly, this preserve is too attractive to hide in the cellar. Offer some of the jars to friends and family.

Wash lemons, cut off stem ends and slice lemons as thinly as possible. A food processor fitted with a thin slicing blade makes quick work of this job.

Combine lemon slices with any seeds and juice and water in a large saucepan. Cover and bring to a boil. Reduce heat and simmer moderately for 1½ hours or until slices are soft and translucent and liquid has an intense lemon flavour. Add chopped rosemary and simmer, uncovered, for 10 minutes.

Transfer mixture to a dampened jelly bag or colander lined with a double thickness of damp fine cheesecloth. Let drip for 4 hours or overnight.

Prepare thirteen 8-ounce (250 mL) jars (see page 127).

Measure the juice; there should be about 12 cups (3 L). Divide juice in half. In a jam pan or large heavy saucepan, combine each portion with an equal volume of sugar. Stirring frequently, boil for about 10 minutes or until jelly stage is reached.

Remove from heat and skim off scum. Pour into jars, leaving ½-inch (1 cm) headspace. Immediately insert a sprig of rosemary into each jar. Let cool for 30 minutes. If rosemary sprig floats to surface, push back into the jelly; it is prettiest at a diagonal. Seal with wax (see page 128). Wipe jars, cover with clean lids and label. Store in a cool, dark, dry place.

Makes about twelve 8-ounce (250 mL) jars.

Mint Sauce Jelly

When spearmint, peppermint, orange or applemint threatens to take over your garden, gather a bundle and make jelly. It's delicious with lamb, especially barbecued butterflied leg or grilled chops.

12 cups coarsely chopped, unpeeled, uncored apples (12 large)	3 L
2 cups light packed coarsely chopped fresh mint leaves and stems	500 mL
4 cups water	1 L
2 cups cider vinegar	500 mL
Granulated sugar	
2 tbsp very finely chopped fresh mint leaves	25 mL

Combine apples, coarsely chopped mint, water and vinegar in a large saucepan. Bring to a boil. Reduce heat and cook, uncovered, for 30 to 35 minutes or until apples are mushy. Mash periodically to soften apples and bruise mint.

Transfer mixture to a dampened jelly bag or a colander lined with a double thickness of damp fine cheesecloth. Let drip for 4 hours or overnight.

Prepare seven 8-ounce (250 mL) jars (see page 127).

Measure juice; there should be about 7 cups (1.75 L). Divide in half. Combine each portion with an equal volume of sugar in a jam pan or heavy saucepan and bring to a boil. Stirring constantly, boil vigorously for about 10 minutes or until jelly stage is reached.

Remove from heat and skim off scum. Stir in finely chopped mint, continuing to stir for 3 minutes to distribute mint in the cooling jelly. Pour into jars, leaving ½-inch (1 cm) headspace. Let cool for 10 minutes. Seal with wax (see page 128). Wipe jars, cover with clean lids and label. Store in a cool, dark, dry place.

Makes about six 8-ounce (250 mL) jars.

Spicy Hot Chili Sauce

16 cups chopped, peeled tomatoes (about 24 large)	4 L
4 cups chopped, peeled, cored apples (4 large)	1 L
3¼ cups firmly packed brown sugar	800 mL
3 cups cider vinegar	750 mL
1 cup chopped onion	250 mL
1 cup chopped sweet green pepper (1 large)	250 mL
1 cup chopped sweet red pepper (1 large)	250 mL
⅓ cup chopped hot red pepper (1 medium)	75 mL
2 cloves garlic, minced	2
1 tbsp each allspice, mustard seed and pickling salt	15 mL
1½ tsp cinnamon	7 mL
¼ tsp freshly grated nutmeg	1 mL
¼ tsp cayenne	1 mL

This chili sauce is a slight departure from the classic version. It has lots of allspice and cinnamon, as well as apples that break down to make a smooth base for the pieces of tomato, onion and pepper.

Prepare eight 16-ounce (500 mL) preserving jars and lids (see page 127).

Combine all the ingredients in a large preserving kettle and bring to a boil. Reduce heat and simmer, stirring frequently, for about 2 hours or until sauce is thick and dark rich red in colour.

Pour into jars, leaving ¼-inch (5 mm) headspace. Immediately seal with disks and bands. Let cool, wipe and label. Store in a cool, dark, dry place.

Makes seven or eight 16-ounce (500 mL) jars.

Zucchini Confetti Relish

8 cups finely chopped zucchini (about 3 lb/1.35 kg)	2 L
2 cups finely chopped onions (4 medium)	500 mL
1 cup finely chopped sweet red pepper (1 large)	250 mL
½ cup finely chopped green pepper	125 mL
¼ cup pickling salt	50 mL
2½ cups granulated sugar	625 mL
1½ cups white vinegar	375 mL
1½ tsp dry mustard	7 mL
1 tsp celery seed	5 mL
½ tsp coarsely ground pepper	2 mL
½ tsp turmeric	2 mL
2 tsp cornstarch	10 mL
1 tbsp water	15 mL

A great quick relish for hot dogs. Make fast work of chopping the zucchini and onions in a food processor if you have one, but chop the peppers by hand for neat little cubes that look like confetti among the other vegetables.

Prepare seven 8-ounce (250 mL) preserving jars and lids (see page 127).

Combine zucchini, onions, red and green peppers in a large bowl and sprinkle with salt. Stir to distribute the salt evenly. Let stand for 1 to 2 hours, stirring periodically. Drain, rinse thoroughly under cold running water and drain again, pressing out excess moisture.

In a large heavy saucepan or preserving kettle, combine the sugar, vinegar, mustard, celery seed, pepper and turmeric. Bring to a boil; add drained vegetables and bring back to a boil, stirring frequently. Reduce heat and simmer, uncovered, for 25 minutes or until the vegetables are tender and the sauce thickened.

In a small bowl, stir together the cornstarch and water and mix into the relish. Cook, stirring constantly, until clear, about 5 minutes.

Pour into jars, leaving ¼-inch (5 mm) headspace. Immediately seal with disks and bands. Let cool, wipe and label. Store in a cool, dark, dry spot.

Makes about six 8-ounce (250 mL) jars.

Gingery Orange and Peach Chutney

4 cups chopped peaches (6 large peaches)	1 L
2 cups chopped onions (4 medium)	500 mL
1½ cups golden raisins	375 mL
1½ cups granulated sugar	375 mL

Good with barbecued chicken or ham steaks.

Prepare five 8-ounce (250 mL) preserving jars and lids (see page 127).

Combine all ingredients except preserved ginger in a large saucepan. Bring to a boil. Reduce heat and simmer for

- 2 tsp salt — 10 mL
- 1 tbsp grated fresh ginger — 15 mL
- 1 tsp each cinnamon and allspice — 5 mL
- 1/4 tsp freshly grated nutmeg — 1 mL
- 2 tbsp grated orange peel — 25 mL
- 2/3 cup orange juice — 150 mL
- 1 1/2 cups cider vinegar — 375 mL
- 1/3 cup chopped preserved ginger — 75 mL

1 1/2 to 2 hours or until thick, smooth and a rich golden brown, stirring frequently to prevent scorching. About 15 minutes before the end of the cooking time, add the preserved ginger.

Ladle chutney into jars, leaving 1/4-inch (5 mm) headspace. Immediately cover with disks and bands. Let cool, wipe and label. Store in a cool, dark, dry place.

Makes about four 8-ounce (250 mL) jars.

Apple Tomato Mint Chutney

In all my years of making preserves, few chutneys have equalled this mild fruity one. It's great with barbecued meat, poultry and semi-hard cheeses.

- 7 cups chopped, peeled, cored apples (7 large) — 1.75 L
- 3 1/2 cups chopped onions (7 medium) — 875 mL
- 3 1/2 cups chopped peeled tomatoes (7 medium) — 875 mL
- 2 cups raisins — 500 mL
- 1 tbsp grated orange peel — 15 mL
- 1/2 cup orange juice — 125 mL
- 1 tbsp grated lemon peel — 15 mL
- 1/3 cup lemon juice — 75 mL
- 3 1/2 cups granulated sugar — 875 mL
- 2 cups cider vinegar — 500 mL
- 1 tsp salt — 5 mL
- 2/3 cup finely chopped fresh mint — 150 mL
- 1/4 cup finely chopped fresh parsley — 50 mL

Prepare nine 8-ounce (250 mL) preserving jars and lids (see page 127).

Combine all ingredients in a large heavy saucepan or preserving kettle and bring to a gentle boil over medium-high heat, stirring frequently. Reduce heat and simmer until thick, about 1 1/2 hours.

Ladle into jars, leaving 1/4-inch (5 mm) headspace. Immediately seal with disks and bands. Let cool, wipe and label. Store in cool, dark, dry place.

Makes about eight 8-ounce (250 mL) jars.

Pear and Ginger Chutney with Apricots

2 large oranges	2	
1 cup water	250 mL	
1 cup sliced dried apricots (5 oz/150 g)	250 mL	
12 cups chopped pears (11 large), about 5 lb (2.25 kg)	3 L	
1½ cups chopped onions (3 medium)	375 mL	
⅓ cup grated or finely chopped fresh ginger	75 mL	
2½ cups granulated sugar	625 mL	
1½ cups golden raisins	375 mL	
1¼ cups white vinegar	300 mL	
1½ tsp salt	7 mL	
1 tsp mustard seed	5 mL	
½ tsp each ground coriander, cumin and cinnamon	2 mL	
¼ tsp ground allspice	1 mL	
Pinch cayenne	Pinch	
¾ cup chopped preserved ginger	175 mL	

This golden tangy chutney is a natural with turkey, goose, ham or pork. It is also excellent with rich pâtés or with crackers and mild creamy cheeses. Buy hard pears and let them ripen for one to three days, at room temperature and out of direct sunlight, until they are fragrant and somewhat juicy, but still firm. You can speed up the ripening by putting them in a paper bag.

Prepare ten 8-ounce (250 mL) preserving jars and lids (see page 127).

Wash oranges. With a very sharp paring knife, remove zest (thin outer peel) from one of the oranges and cut enough of it into fine slivers to make ½ cup (125 mL). Squeeze oranges and reserve juice. Place measured orange peel and water in a small saucepan; cover and simmer until peel is tender, about 15 minutes. Add apricots; cover and simmer for 10 minutes or until apricots are softened and puffed.

Meanwhile, in a large heavy saucepan, combine the orange juice with the pears and onions. Tie the fresh ginger in a double thickness of fine cheesecloth. Add to the pan along with sugar, raisins, vinegar, salt, mustard seed, coriander, cumin, cinnamon, allspice and cayenne. Pour in orange-apricot mixture and stir.

Bring to a boil, uncovered, over medium heat. Reduce heat and simmer, stirring frequently, until chutney has thickened, about 1 hour. Remove bag of fresh ginger, pressing out any juices. Add preserved ginger and simmer for 10 to 15 minutes or until the ingredients have blended together, stirring almost constantly and reducing heat if necessary to prevent scorching.

Pour into jars, leaving ¼-inch (5 mm) headspace. Immediately seal with disks and bands. Let cool, wipe and label. Store in cool, dark, dry place.

Makes nine 8-ounce (250 mL) jars plus a generous taster.

Spiced Pickled Pears in Port

½ cup port	125 mL
½ cup red wine vinegar or cider vinegar	125 mL
½ cup water	125 mL
⅔ cup granulated sugar	150 mL
10 whole cloves	10
1 cinnamon stick, broken apart	1
2 lb pears	1 kg

Spiced fruits are an excellent garnish for ham, pork loin, duck or goose. Or serve in a glass dish with the port-wine poaching liquid, to complement a slice of pâté or an array of cold meats.

Combine port, vinegar, water, sugar and spices in a medium saucepan. Cover and bring to a boil. Reduce heat and simmer for 5 minutes.

Peel and halve the pears. Core carefully with a melon baller or 1 tsp (5 mL) measuring spoon. Arrange curved side up in the spiced liquid, cover and bring to a boil. Reduce heat and simmer for 10 minutes. Gently turn pears, cover and poach for 10 minutes longer. Uncover and simmer for 10 to 15 minutes or until the pears are tender but not mushy and the liquid has evaporated to about 1 cup (250 mL).

Let cool and store in a jar or airtight plastic container in the refrigerator for up to 2 weeks. Makes about 1 quart (1 L).

Pickled Herbed Mushrooms

2 lb button mushrooms	1 kg
$\frac{1}{4}$ cup lemon juice	50 mL
6 cups water	1.5 L
$1\frac{1}{2}$ tsp salt	7 mL
2 cups white wine vinegar	500 mL
$\frac{1}{2}$ cup olive oil	125 mL
2 tsp chopped fresh thyme or 1 tsp (5 mL) crumbled dried	10 mL
1 tsp coarsely ground pepper	5 mL
2 bay leaves	2

Choose the smallest, whitest and firmest mushrooms for pickling. Serve the final product on an antipasto tray with salami, olives, cherry tomatoes and pickled peppers.

Prepare two 16-ounce (500 mL) preserving jars and lids (see page 127).

Trim mushrooms. Rinse briefly in cold water, shake off excess moisture and immediately pat dry. Place in a large saucepan with lemon juice, water and salt. Cover, bring to a gentle boil and simmer for 6 minutes. Drain, discarding liquid.

Meanwhile, combine vinegar, oil, thyme and pepper in a saucepan and heat to boiling. Pack mushrooms into prepared jars, leaving $\frac{1}{2}$-inch (1 cm) headspace. Cover with boiling vinegar; add a bay leaf to each jar. Press out air bubbles and add more liquid to cover mushrooms completely, leaving $\frac{1}{4}$-inch (5 mm) headspace. Immediately seal with disks and bands. Let cool, wipe and label. Store in a cool, dark, dry place for at least 1 week before serving.

Makes about two 16-ounce (500 mL) jars.

Pickled Silverskin Onions with Horseradish

8 cups small silverskin onions (3¼ lb/1.5 kg)	2 L
Boiling water	
½ cup pickling salt	125 mL
Cold water	

PICKLING LIQUID:

1 cup granulated sugar	250 mL
4 cups white vinegar	1 L
2 tbsp mustard seed	25 mL
4 tsp grated horseradish	20 mL
6 bay leaves	6
3 small dried hot red peppers, halved	3

Covering silverskin onions with boiling water makes the task of peeling them less tedious. The dollop of horseradish is what makes this pickle superior.

Place onions in a heatproof bowl. Cover with boiling water and let stand for 2 minutes. Drain, refresh under cold running water and peel. Sprinkle with pickling salt and cover with cold water. Stir well, cover lightly and let stand for 12 hours or overnight. Drain, rinse well and set aside. Prepare seven 8-ounce (250 mL) jars and lids (see page 127).

PICKLING LIQUID: In a medium saucepan, combine sugar, vinegar, mustard seed and horseradish. Bring to a boil, reduce heat and simmer, uncovered, for 5 minutes.

Add onions and simmer, uncovered, for about 10 minutes or until onions are translucent but still very crisp. Pour immediately into prepared jars, leaving ¼-inch (5 mm) headspace and making sure the onions are covered with pickling liquid. Add a bay leaf and half a hot red pepper to each jar. Immediately seal with disks and bands. Let cool, wipe and label. Store for about 1 month in a cool, dark, dry place for the flavours to mellow.

Makes about six 8-ounce (250 mL) jars.

Golden Mustard Pickles

1½ lb small silverskin pickling onions (4 cups/1 L)	750 g
1 quart very small cucumbers (1 lb/500 g)	1 L
2 sweet red bell peppers (6 oz/175 g each)	2
1 cauliflower (1 lb/500 g)	1
¾ cup pickling salt	175 mL
8 cups cold water	2 L
2½ cups granulated sugar	625 mL
½ cup all-purpose flour	125 mL
½ cup dry mustard	125 mL
2 tbsp celery seed	25 mL
2 tsp turmeric	10 mL
4 cups cider vinegar	1 L

What makes this mustard pickle special is its chunkiness and piquancy. Whole silverskin onions, tiny cucumbers, cauliflower florets and strips of red pepper are pickled in a tangy mustard sauce. It's best served with cold meats, especially ham. If, by chance, there is a spoonful of sauce left in the bottom of the jar, add it to a fall cabbage salad.

Prepare the vegetables. To peel tiny onions, cover them with boiling water and let stand for 2 minutes. Drain, rinse in cold water and peel. Scrub cucumbers, removing the prickles and stems. If your cucumbers are larger than gherkins, cut into ¾-inch (2 cm) pieces. Cut the peppers into strips ½ inch (1 cm) wide and 2½ inches (6 cm) long. Divide the cauliflower into small florets.

Place vegetables in layers in a large bowl or crock, sprinkling salt between the layers. Pour water over vegetables. Cover lightly and let stand overnight. Drain, rinse and drain again. Prepare six 16-ounce (500 mL) preserving jars and lids (see page 127).

Combine the sugar, flour, mustard, celery seed and turmeric in a large saucepan or preserving kettle. Blend in vinegar a little at a time to prevent lumps from forming. Place over moderate heat and cook until thickened, stirring constantly. Add vegetables and simmer for 15 minutes, stirring frequently.

Pour into prepared jars, leaving a ¼-inch (5 mm) headspace and making sure the sauce covers the vegetables. Immediately seal with disks and bands. Let cool, wipe and label. Store in cool, dark, dry place.

Makes about five 16-ounce (500 mL) jars.

Herbed Tomato Sauce

$\frac{1}{3}$ cup olive oil	75 mL
$1\frac{1}{2}$ cups chopped celery (2 stalks)	375 mL
1 cup chopped carrots (2 medium)	250 mL
1 cup chopped onions (2 medium)	250 mL
1 large clove garlic, minced	1
6 quarts plum or beefsteak tomatoes (9 lb/4 kg)	6 L
2 tsp each chopped fresh basil and oregano or 1 tsp (5 mL) crumbled dried	10 mL
1 tsp granulated sugar	5 mL
$\frac{1}{2}$ tsp salt	2 mL
$\frac{1}{4}$ tsp freshly ground pepper	1 mL
$\frac{1}{4}$ tsp fennel seeds	1 mL
1 bay leaf	1

A pot of fresh tomato sauce ranks high among the preserves you can make for the winter. With a bowl of pasta and freshly grated Parmesan, you have a quick and delicious supper. Spoon it over grilled cod steaks, stuff it into a simple omelet, or use it as a sauce for steamed cauliflower or beans. It's hard to run out of ideas for this favourite summery sauce. Freeze the sauce in convenient containers.

In a large saucepan, heat oil over moderate heat. Add celery, carrots, onions and garlic and fry until tender but not browned, about 15 minutes.

Wash, trim and core tomatoes. Chop coarsely and add to the pan. Bring to a simmer and cook, mashing periodically, until vegetables are tender, 45 to 60 minutes.

Pass through a food mill using a medium disk or through a conical ricer. Return purée to a large deep clean saucepan. Add all other ingredients and simmer for $1\frac{1}{2}$ to 2 hours or until thick, stirring frequently.

Pour sauce into airtight containers, leaving $\frac{1}{2}$-inch (1 cm) headspace and freeze.

Makes about twelve 8-ounce (250 mL) containers.

INDEX

Other Books in the Great Canadian Cookbook Series

Summer Berries

Elizabeth Baird

A superb collection of recipes that does mouth-watering justice to Canada's wide assortment of delicious berries.

Apples, Peaches & Pears

Elizabeth Baird

Over 100 recipes, from the classic to the most inventive, for three of Canada's finest fruits.

Classic Canadian Cooking

Elizabeth Baird

An attractive guide to the Canadian cooking tradition, with over 300 recipes organized by the season in which their ingredients are at their finest and most plentiful.

Rose Murray's Vegetable Cookbook

Thirty-one vegetables widely available in Canada are feted in 132 recipes for soups, appetizers, salads, main dishes and desserts.

The Christmas Cookbook

Rose Murray

The indispensable aid to food lovers and cooks who want to enjoy a culinary Christmas.

A Taste of the Wild

Blanche Pownall Garrett

Imaginative and intriguing recipes using 42 wild plants and fruits found in most parts of the country.

Canadian Country Preserves & Wines

Blanche Pownall Garrett

Fine recipes and the lore of preserving both garden produce and wild plants.

Kids in the Kitchen

Shannon Ferrier

A cookbook designed especially for kids 6 to 8, with attractive line drawings and instructions that are easily understood.

More Kids in the Kitchen

Shannon Ferrier and Tamara Shuttleworth

Over 40 nutritious and delicious recipes for kids 10 and up who have discovered the fun and satisfaction of learning to cook.

The KidsFood Cookbook

Shannon Ferrier and Tamara Shuttleworth

This book shows how to make "take-out" treats at home. Everything from hamburgers and pizza to tacos and egg rolls is included.

The Kids' Bakebook

Shannon Ferrier and Tamara Shuttleworth

The latest from Canada's premier children's cookbook authors introduces the basics of baking and presents an appetizing selection of recipes for cookies, cakes, muffins, biscuits, yeast breads and quick breads.